Cut Out +

LAURENCE KING

Published in 2015
by Laurence King Publishing Ltd
361–373 City Road
London EC1V 1LR
United Kingdom
Tel: + 44 20 7841 6900
Fax: +44 20 7841 6910
e-mail: enquiries@laurenceking.com
www.laurenceking.com

A catalogue record for this book is available
from the British Library.

ISBN: 978-1-78067-416-2

Design and line drawings by Evelin Kasikov.
Cover photography by Ida Riveros.

Printed in Hong Kong

Cat Morley & Tom Waddington

Cut Out + Keep

AROUND THE USA
IN 50 CRAFT PROJECTS

Laurence King Publishing

Contents

INtRoDuctioN

In June 2011, we set out on an epic road trip with the aim of driving through every state in America while taking travel advice from the members of our website, Cut Out + Keep. Covering 50 states in just eight months, we lived out of suitcases, hopping between motels and working from coffee shops.

We soaked up the culture as we passed through each of the states, making friends, trying the food, and having the journey of a lifetime. Inspired by our adventures and the amazing diversity of the country, this book is a collection of our stories from the road, along with craft projects for each state.

Cut Out + Keep started as Cat's personal blog while she was studying at college in 2003. She shared photos of the crafts she was making, along with step-by-step instructions. The blog became popular, which gave us the idea to transform the site into a community where everyone could share projects. At the time of writing the site boasts more than 60,000 projects and 170,000 members worldwide, with the majority in America.

PLEASE
DO NOT CLIMB
ON THE GATOR

When we started Cut Out + Keep in rainy Scotland, we never could have imagined how big it would grow, and that members on the other side of the world would be sharing projects. We had never visited America before, and knew very little about each of the states, so we spent the first few months excitedly watching as members from exotic-sounding cities like Minneapolis, San Antonio, and Sedona shared their projects and gave us an insight into where they came from. As the membership grew, so did our curiosity about each of the states—what they were like to live in and, even more importantly, what it was like to craft in them. It soon became a shared dream to visit America one day.

At the end of 2010, Tom was able to quit his day job and work on the site full-time. With the option of working from anywhere in the world, we realized it was the perfect opportunity to head out on an adventure. We booked plane tickets, packed our bags, and set off. We started out in Omaha, Nebraska, in the very middle of the country. Being in the heart of the Midwest certainly helped us get sucked into the American way of life, and everyone was incredibly welcoming and happy to help.

Our road trip was one of the most amazing and inspiring experiences we've ever had. We ate new kinds of food, met amazing people, visited incredible sights. The thing that struck us most was how unique each of the states was. They all had something that made them special.

We've taken inspiration from our time in each state—the food, the landmarks, the culture, and even the claims to fame—and translated them into simple, fun tutorials you can try at home. Each project is designed to introduce you to a new craft, and we've tried to reuse the same materials over and over again, so you can give a few a go at the same time. Even if you've never had a chance to visit, you'll already have a souvenir, and we hope this book will inspire you to set out on your own adventures and craft something wonderful when you return.

So, buckle up, and let's get this show on the road!

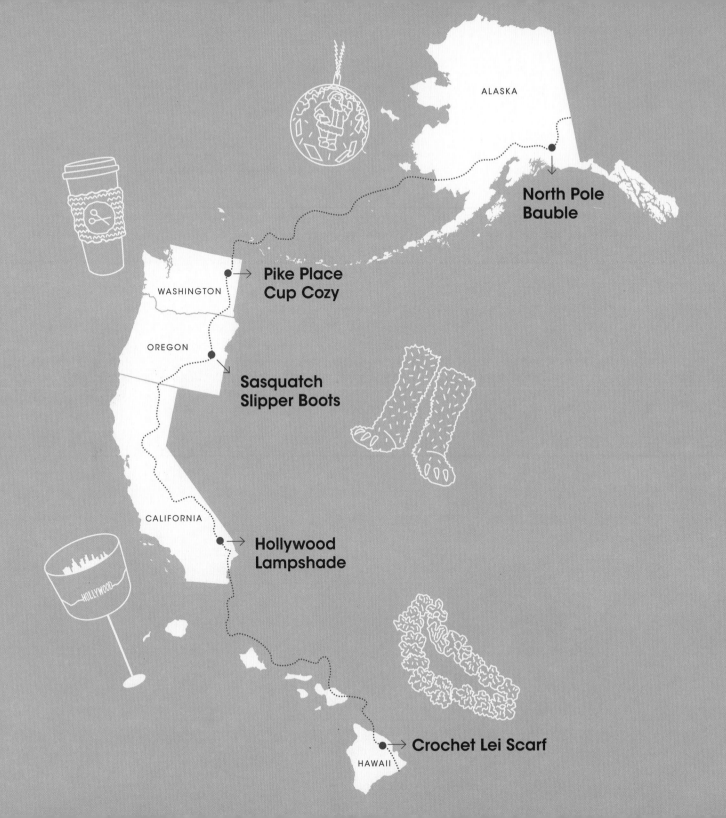

North Pole Bauble

Pike Place Cup Cozy

ALASKA

WASHINGTON

OREGON

Sasquatch Slipper Boots

CALIFORNIA

Hollywood Lampshade

HOLLYWOOD

Crochet Lei Scarf

HAWAII

Traveling through the Denali countryside on the Alaska Railroad.

"The First Unknown Family" statue, Golden Heart Park, Fairbanks.

The Kenai Mountains from the Seward Highway.

Aurora Ice Museum, Chena Hot Springs.

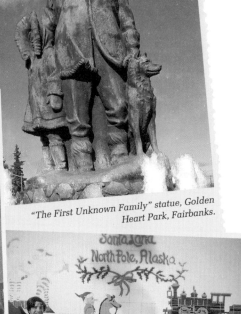
Riding Santa's sleigh in North Pole.

Designated driver at Silver Gulch Brewery.

Abandoned seven-story igloo-shaped hotel on the George Parks Highway.

ALASKA

Known as the Last Frontier, Alaska is more than twice the size of Texas but has less than 0.3 percent of its population. We started our adventure by taking the scenic *Alaska Railroad* up to *Fairbanks*, a city so far north that you have to look in all directions for a chance of seeing the *aurora borealis* (northern lights). We took in the local history at the *Dog Mushers Museum* downtown before going to see the start of the gigantic *Trans-Alaska Pipeline System* in nearby *Fox* and grabbing a bite to eat at the *Silver Gulch*, America's most northern brewery.

From there, we drove south to a town named *North Pole*, where you can pose with a giant Santa, meet his reindeer, and pick up decorations in the Christmas store.

The best time of year to visit Alaska is March, when the state retains its winter charm without the extreme conditions. However, you can get a taste of winter magic all year round at the *Aurora Ice Museum*, where you can sip an appletini in a glass made from ice while admiring dozens of impressive ice sculptures. We warmed up in the *Chena Hot Springs* afterward, while waiting for sunset and a chance of seeing the northern lights.

Leaving Fairbanks, we drove south through the town of *Nenana*, where betting on the Ice Classic awards a jackpot to whoever predicts exactly when the winter ice will break up in the Nenana River. Down in the wilderness of *Denali National Park and Preserve* we tried to spot the elusive *Mount McKinley*, the highest mountain in North America. The weather system around the mountain means that it's often under clouds, so only 10 percent of tourists actually manage to see it.

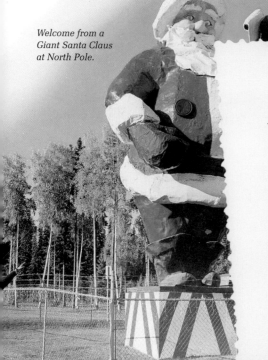

Welcome from a Giant Santa Claus at North Pole.

POST | CARD

We grabbed breakfast at the *City Diner (3000 Minnesota Drive)* in *Anchorage* and stopped off to see a snow-plowing train before heading south to *Chugach National Forest*, where we got to walk (carefully, it's slippy!) on *Byron Glacier*. If you're not lucky enough to spy any animals in the wild, you can see a huge selection of rescued wildlife, including bears, elk, and moose, at the *Alaska Wildlife Conservation Center* in *Girdwood*.

We ended our trip in *Seward* on the coast, where you can catch sightseeing cruises out to the Pacific Ocean, or sample fresh seafood in the harbor. We tucked into Alaskan salmon quesadillas at the *Railway Cantina (1401 4th Ave.)* before spending the night in a cozy yurt at *Sourdough Sue's (33940 Tressler Ave.)* on Bear Lake.

North Pole Bauble

With all letters to Santa heading to North Pole, AK, this bauble will remind you of all those wishlists at Christmas time.

STEP 1 Splatter the top of the bauble with the nail polish.

YOU WILL NEED

Clear plastic bauble
Glow-in-the-dark nail polish
Seasonal photograph
Paper
Hot-glue gun
String

STEP 2 When you're happy with the design, set it aside to dry.

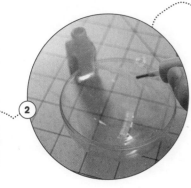

STEP 3 Print out your photo twice, and cut the bottom part off one. Repeat the same process with a mirrored version of the photo.

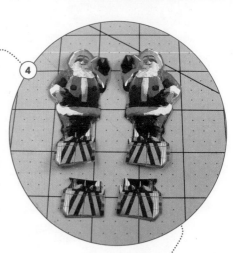

STEP 4 Stick the photos and reverse photos together. Make a slit in the bottom of the full image and an equal-sized slit in the top of the half-image.

STEP 5 Slot the pieces together to create a stand-up image.

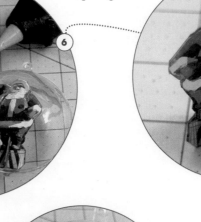

STEP 6 Hot-glue the photo along the bottom and stick inside the bauble.

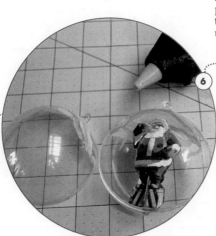

STEP 7 Cut out lots of mini envelopes and stick the flaps together with glue.

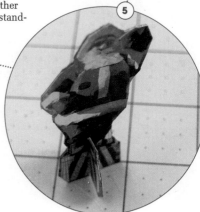

STEP 8 Address each of the letters to Santa.

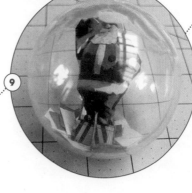

STEP 9 Fill the bauble with mini letters and attach a length of string so you can hang it on your Christmas tree.

Chewing gum stuck on the walls of Post Alley, Seattle.

Milk-bottle-shaped building, Spokane.

Animated neon sign in Seattle

At the XXX Rootbeer Drive-In.

Staying in a vintage trailer at the Sou'wester Lodge.

Meeting a kangaroo at Outback, Washington.

Spelling practice in Riverfront Park, Spokane.

Kurt Cobain's memorial in his hometown, Aberdeen.

WASHINGTON

We made our way past the six-story-high *Peace Arch* at the Canadian border into Washington, as an eerie fog hung over the dense pine trees. Hidden in the forest, *The Outback Kangaroo and Christmas Tree Farm* in *Arlington* might sound like an odd combination, but it's the ideal place to get up close to wildlife, kiss an alpaca, and cradle a baby 'roo.

We then headed to *Seattle*, where we picked up a coffee from the first *Starbucks* store (opened in 1971) and a freshly made crumpet from *The Crumpet Shop (1503 1st Ave.)*, before exploring the numerous stalls in *Pike Place Market*. If you're feeling brave, a trip past the chewing-gum-covered Gum Wall at *Post Alley* is sure to make your stomach turn, especially on a hot, sticky day!

Slightly less scary, the *Fremont Troll* sculpture sits underneath the Aurora Bridge and makes for a great photo op. *Archie McPhee (1300 N. 45th St.)* is the perfect place for quirky souvenirs, before some pinball and ice cream at *Full Tilt (4759 Brooklyn Ave. NE)*. You'll spot the famous *Space Needle* from all across the city, or head up the landmark itself for a 360-degree view.

We also took a trip through *North Bend* and *Twin Falls* (the setting for the TV series *Twin Peaks*), and drove through the town of *George, Washington*, a fun play on the state's namesake. In *Spokane*, *Riverfront Park* is full of unusual sculptures, including a trash-eating goat, and offers a cable-car ride over the river and waterfalls. We had breakfast at *Frank's (1516 W. 2nd Ave.)*, an old, ornate railcar that is now a diner.

In *Issaquah*, the *XXX Rootbeer Drive-in (98 NE Gilman Blvd.)* is full of crazy kitsch Americana, and huge milkshakes! Over on the coast, the childhood home of Kurt Cobain in *Aberdeen* still attracts visitors. We spent the night nearby in an incredible shiny 1950s trailer home next to *Seaview* at *Sou'wester Lodge (3728 J Pl.)*.

Pike Place Market, downtown Seattle.

Pike Place Cup Cozy

Seattle is well known for coffee, but not the warmest of weather. This cup cozy will keep your latte hot while showing off your crafting skills.

YOU WILL NEED

Worsted-weight (aran) yarn
Patch, button, or embellishment
Size 8 (5mm) knitting needles
Yarn needle
Needle and thread

This project uses US terminology. For a table of UK terms, please see page 240.

STEP 1
Knit the cozy.

Note: The top 6 and bottom 6 rows are worked in a 2 x 2 variation of seed stitch. The middle section is worked in stockinette stitch. We chose to keep the "wrong" (the purl) side on the outside. The cozy tapers slightly so it will fit the cup snugly.

Cast on 46 stitches.
Rows 1–6: (K2, p2) to last 2 sts, k2.
Row 7: (RS) Purl.
Row 8: Knit, decreasing 1 st at each side. (44 sts)
Row 9: Purl.
Row 10: Knit.
Row 11: Purl.
Row 12: Knit, decreasing 1 st at each side. (42 sts)
Row 13: Purl.
Row 14: Knit.
Row 15: Purl.
Rows 16–21: (K2, p2) to last 2 sts, k2.
Bind (cast) off.

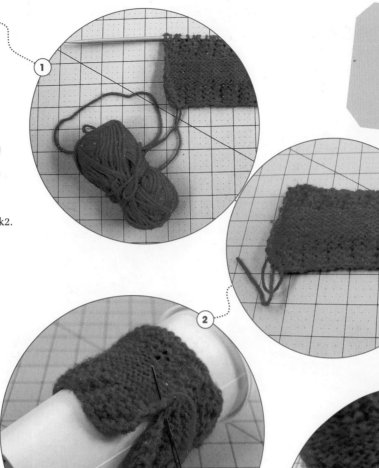

TIP

Leave a long tail of yarn when you bind off. Use it to sew the edges together.

STEP 2 Wrap your cozy around your coffee cup and check the fit. Using a yarn needle, sew the two edges together.

STEP 3 Pick out a cute patch, button, or embellishment to personalize your cozy, and stitch it on.

NOTE

Our cozy measured 3 x 9in (7.5 x 23cm). If you want to make your cozy for a bigger or smaller cup, adjust the pattern by adding or removing two stitches.

Roosevelt elk roadblock on the Redwood Highway.

The 24 Hour Church of Elvis in Portland.

The world's smallest park at Mill Ends Park, Portland.

Our treehouse at the Out 'n' About Treesort.

Treats at Voodoo Doughnut, Portland.

Roadside Bigfoot tree sculpture.

Carved tree at Out 'n' About Treesort.

Oregon

Oregon is known for doing things a little differently, so when a giant sign told us to "Keep Portland Weird," we knew we were in for a fun time. *Voodoo Doughnut (22 SW 3rd Ave.)*, painted in glittering pink, manages to have a huge queue for its sparkly, cereal-covered donuts all day long—unless it's closed for a wedding.

POST | CARD

The city is full of art, artists, and unusual finds—the *24 Hour Church of Elvis* was full of coin-operated interactive trinkets, *Powell's Books (1005 W. Burnside St.)* claims to be the world's largest second-hand bookstore, while *Mill Ends Park (SW Taylor St.)* is the world's smallest park (only 2ft/60cm wide) and is the "only leprechaun colony west of Ireland"!

Making our way through the forest and wilderness, we kept an eye out for Bigfoot, who's frequently spotted throughout the state and Pacific Northwest. However, our best wildlife sighting was a giant herd of Roosevelt elk. They're only found in this area of the world, and they caused a huge traffic jam as they collectively decided to cross the road at their own leisurely pace.

In the south of the state, the *Oregon Caves* are huge underground halls made of marble. The night we spent at the *Out 'n' About Treesort (300 Page Creek Rd.)* in *Cave Junction* was one of the most enjoyable of the trip, with its collection of incredible hand-built treehouses in the forest. We weren't the first to check in to our room that night, though—a squirrel was waiting for us on our arrival!

Portland Rule #1—Keep Portland Weird.

Sasquatch Slipper Boots

Just like Bigfoot keeps warm in the woods, you'll keep warm around the house with these cozy boots.

YOU WILL NEED

Paper
Quilted lining fabric
Furry fabric
Polymer clay
Glow-in-the-dark paint
Sewing machine
Awl
Paintbrush
Needle and thread

Create the pattern

Each boot is made from three shapes, so start by making a template for each. The first is a long, tapered pipe for the leg. Measure your calf and ankle, divide these numbers in half, then trace the shape of your leg on paper, adding 1in (2.5cm) around the whole piece for extra room. The second piece is the bottom of the boot. Trace around your foot on paper and add 1in (2.5cm) around the whole foot. The final piece is for the top of the foot and is the same shape as the front of the bottom, cut at the point where your foot meets your leg.

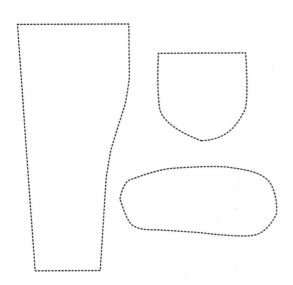

Add a ⅝in (1.5cm) seam allowance to each of these pieces and cut them out.

Cut out the pieces

From the lining fabric:
Cut 4 x leg pieces (with two reversed), 4 x foot bottoms, and 2 x foot tops.

From the furry fabric:
Cut 4 x leg pieces (with two reversed) and 2 x foot tops.

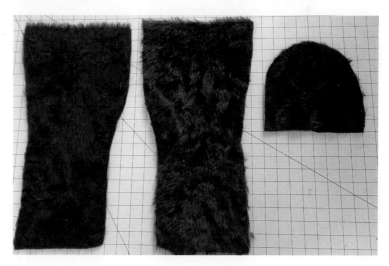

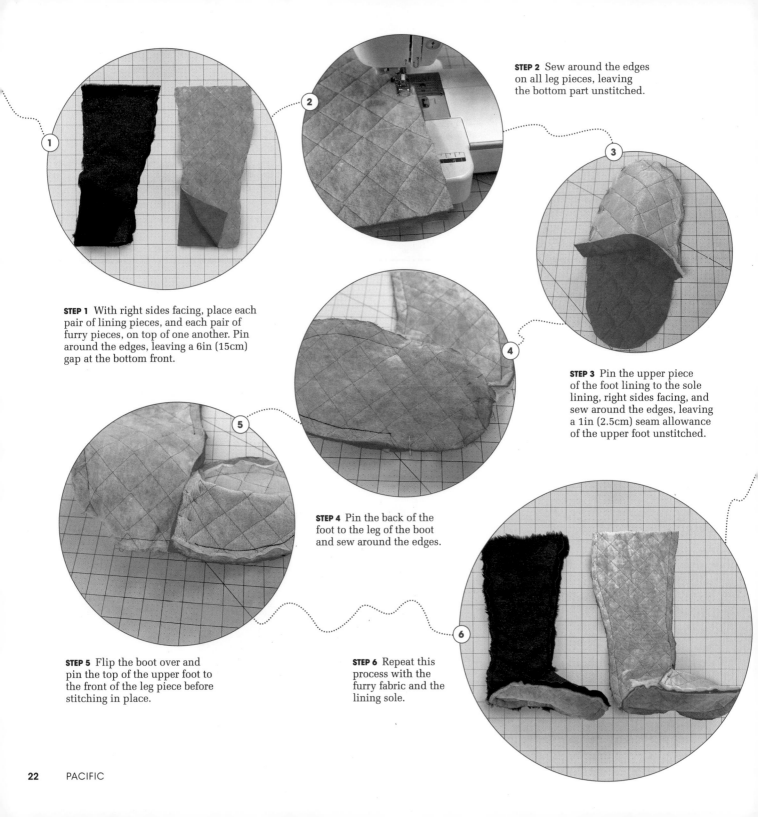

STEP 1 With right sides facing, place each pair of lining pieces, and each pair of furry pieces, on top of one another. Pin around the edges, leaving a 6in (15cm) gap at the bottom front.

STEP 2 Sew around the edges on all leg pieces, leaving the bottom part unstitched.

STEP 3 Pin the upper piece of the foot lining to the sole lining, right sides facing, and sew around the edges, leaving a 1in (2.5cm) seam allowance of the upper foot unstitched.

STEP 4 Pin the back of the foot to the leg of the boot and sew around the edges.

STEP 5 Flip the boot over and pin the top of the upper foot to the front of the leg piece before stitching in place.

STEP 6 Repeat this process with the furry fabric and the lining sole.

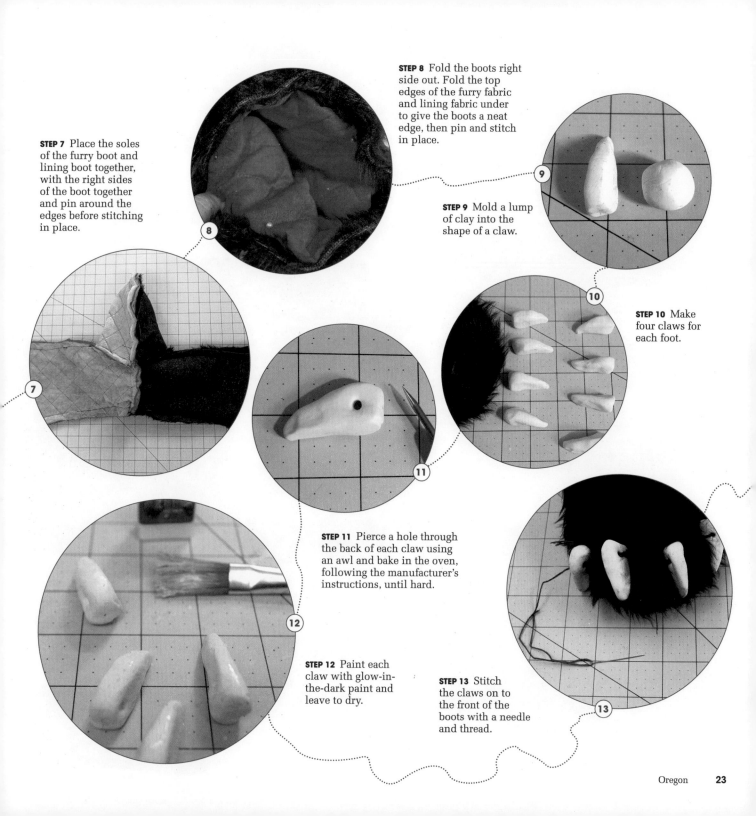

STEP 7 Place the soles of the furry boot and lining boot together, with the right sides of the boot together and pin around the edges before stitching in place.

STEP 8 Fold the boots right side out. Fold the top edges of the furry fabric and lining fabric under to give the boots a neat edge, then pin and stitch in place.

STEP 9 Mold a lump of clay into the shape of a claw.

STEP 10 Make four claws for each foot.

STEP 11 Pierce a hole through the back of each claw using an awl and bake in the oven, following the manufacturer's instructions, until hard.

STEP 12 Paint each claw with glow-in-the-dark paint and leave to dry.

STEP 13 Stitch the claws on to the front of the boots with a needle and thread.

Sunset over Golden Gate Bridge at Vista Point, San Francisco.

One of the sculptures at Peggy Sue's Dinersaur Park.

Visiting the Animaniacs at Warner Bros. Studios, Burbank.

Sleeping in a caboose train car in the Railroad Park Resort, Dunsmuir.

Just squeezing through the Chandelier Tree, Drive-through Tree Park, Leggett.

Sushi burritos from Sushirito, San Francisco.

Hearing sea lions roar at Pier 39, San Francisco.

127 Death Valley Kelbaker Rd

CALIFORNIA

California isn't just stars in the Hollywood Hills, or the hub of technology and startups around San Francisco and the Valley. It's a huge mix of city sprawl and some of the most scenic areas in the country. Its 80,000 farms and ranches account for almost half of all the fruits, nuts, and veg grown in the US, and its vineyards produce eight million bottles of wine per day.

We started our journey in the north. After driving through the *Chandelier Tree*, just off Highway 101, we spent the night at *Railroad Park Resort* in *Dunsmuir*, a collection of train cars transformed into private hotel rooms.

The stars and the tranquility were incredible, and we're sure we can't have been too far from one of the state animals—the bear. Even though the grizzly bear seen on the flag has been extinct here since 1922, black bears still roam free.

We were excited to visit *Silicon Valley*, just south of *San Francisco*'s Bay area, where so many of the tech companies we use every day have made a home— Google, Facebook, Yahoo, and Apple, among others. There's nothing much to see, though, other than office blocks in which new products are being dreamed up. However, downtown is somewhere to give your camera a workout. *Alcatraz* prison is the backdrop to the sea lions at *Pier 39 (39 Concourse)*, next to the recently redeveloped artsy stores in the *Ferry Building*. The trams and steep hills make for postcard-quality snaps, and *Little Italy* and *Chinatown* are bustling with locals and tourists alike.

We also had the chance to catch up with infamous wearable food crocheter, Twinkie Chan, and headed out to the up-and-coming *Mission* district for a bite to eat at vegan Mexican restaurant, *Gracias Madre (2211 Mission St.)*.

Stopping for lunch in Yermo.

The *Golden Gate Bridge* was our last stop. Nothing beats this huge, sweeping structure—it's not surprising that it's one of the most photographed bridges in the world. Then, *In-N-Out Burger* in hand, it was time to get back on the road and head for the bright lights of LA.

Nothing quite prepared us for the energy and diversity of *Los Angeles*. After checking in to the *Hollywood Historic Hotel (5162 Melrose Ave.)*, we headed out for dinner at kitsch hangout, *Swingers Diner (8020 Beverly Blvd.)*. A trip to LA wouldn't be complete without a strut down the *Hollywood Walk of Fame*, comparing hand sizes with the stars at the *Chinese Theatre* (6925 Hollywood Blvd.), celebrity home-spotting on a drive around *Beverly Hills*, and a visit to a movie studio. Just under 300 feature films are produced here every single year. If celebrities aren't your thing, relax with fro-yo on *Venice Beach* or *Malibu* and go hunting for vintage bargains, costumes, and other rare finds at *Hidden Treasures (154 S. Topanga Canyon Blvd.)* in the hills of *Topanga*. For more classic Americana, check out *Frisco's Carhop Diner (18065 E. Gale Ave., City of Industry)* with roller-skating waitresses, or head out to the desert for *Peggy Sue's Diner (35654 W. Yermo Rd.)*, complete with a Dinersaur Park!

Hollywood Lampshade

The Hollywood sign is one of America's most iconic landmarks, shining from the hills above Los Angeles. Inspired by the bright lights of the city, we're going to use the LA skyline to add a bit of sparkle to your home.

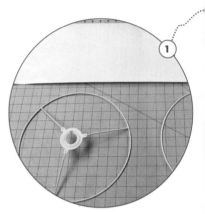

STEP 1 Begin by cutting a piece of white card wide enough to fit around the circumference of your lampshade rings.

YOU WILL NEED

- White card
- Lampshade rings (either from an old lampshade or lampshade kit)
- Paper
- Black card
- Spray adhesive
- Double-sided adhesive tape
- Tracing paper
- Craft knife

GET CREATIVE!

Personalize your lamp by using the skyline of your favorite city or hometown and cut its name into the hills on the reverse side.

STEP 2 Sketch out the skyline of your city, trailing the buildings into a hilly landscape, then Blu-tack it in place on the black card.

STEP 3 Carefully cut out the skyline using a craft knife.

STEP 4 Stick the skyline to the base of the white card using spray adhesive.

STEP 5 Cover the top and bottom lampshade rings with double-sided tape.

STEP 6 Carefully roll the two rings along the top and bottom of your card, so that the skyline is on the inside of the lamp.

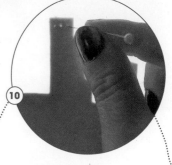

STEP 7 Use another strip of double-sided tape to stick together the two edges of the card.

STEP 8 Sketch the Hollywood sign or your chosen name, Blu-tack in place on the hills, and cut out the letters with the craft knife. Place the inners of the letters to one side.

STEP 9 Glue a piece of tracing paper behind the cut-out letters and carefully glue the inners of the letters back into place.

STEP 10 Attach the shade to a lamp and turn on. Use a pin to prick holes through the lamp for the windows of buildings and lights from the houses.

Sunset on Waikiki Beach.

Tree covered in buoys on the North Shore.

The floating memorial above USS Arizona at Pearl Harbor.

Chocolate haupia pie at Ted's Bakery.

Sea turtles basking on the North Shore.

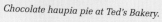

Beet Box Café, North Shore.

Measuring up to a torpedo at Pearl Harbor.

HAWAII

We stayed on *Oahu*, one of the eight major islands that make up the state. Driving around the island, we saw beautiful beaches, roadside coconut stands, and the busy seafront and tourist hotspot of *Waikiki Beach*, where the *Pacific Beach Hotel (2490 Kalakaua Ave.)* has a giant saltwater aquarium with nightly mermaid shows. The Hawaiian language uses only 12 letters, and we loved all the unusual place names. The "pidgin" language then combines the native Hawaiian with English, Portuguese, and Cantonese—*aloha* means both "hello" and "goodbye."

After taking the Kamehameha Highway to see the incredible sea turtles on *Haleiwa Beach*, we headed to the *North Shore*. With waves reaching up to 30ft (9m) high in the winter, it's full of surfers and has a relaxed atmosphere. Food in Hawaii is a mix of American and Asian cuisine, and with so much fresh produce grown right on the island, it's fresh and delicious. On the Kamehameha Highway we cooled off with a rainbow shave ice from *Matsumoto (66–087)*, and tried amazing fresh shrimp from *Mackey's (66–632)*, fresh vegetarian sandwiches from the *Beet Box Café (66–443)*, and chocolate haupia pie from *Ted's Bakery (66–024)*.

Nothing could quite prepare us for the sun, heat, and full-on vacation feeling of the Aloha State. Being fresh off the plane from Alaska (and still wrapped up warm) didn't help!

The *Byodo-In Temple* is a replica of one in Japan, and celebrates the connection between Japan and Hawaii. With koi carp, black swans, and a tranquil atmosphere, it's a great place to visit. You can also get lost in the world's biggest maze at the *Dole Pineapple Plantation*, or head out to sea on one of the many boat excursions. The sunken USS Arizona at *Pearl Harbor* is a memorial to the 1,177 soldiers who lost their lives here in 1941; with the ship visible below the crystal-clear water, and still leaking oil, it's a solemn place to reflect on the events. Even today, sailors who were on the ship are choosing to have their final resting place on board with their crew mates.

On our final night we caught the hula performance by firelight back at Waikiki. We were sad to leave; we'd love to return to see the volcanoes on *Hawaii*, and soak up some more sunshine.

Posing as a Matsumoto rainbow shave ice.

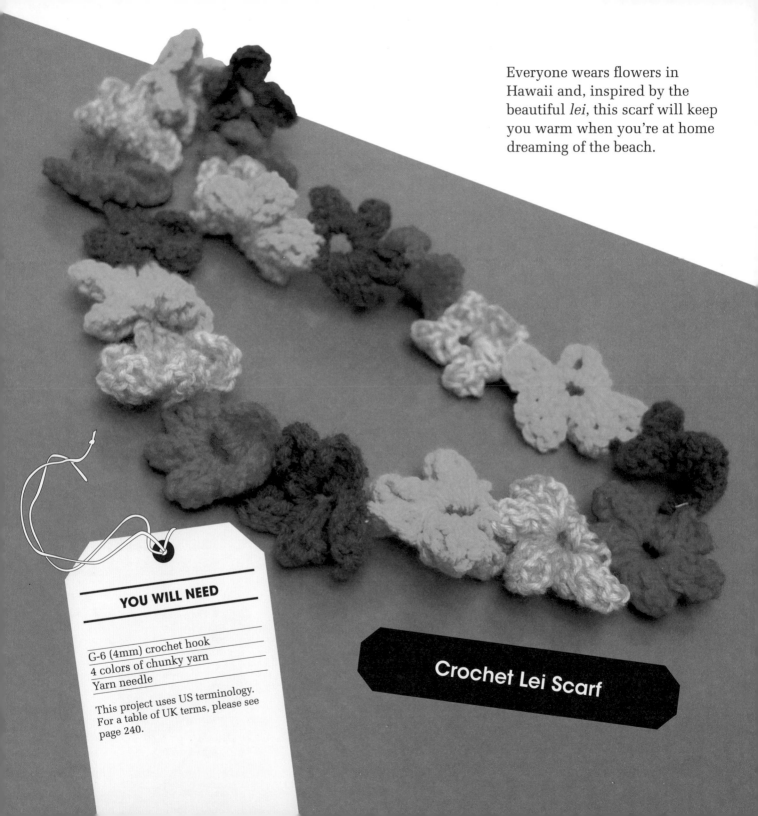

Everyone wears flowers in Hawaii and, inspired by the beautiful *lei*, this scarf will keep you warm when you're at home dreaming of the beach.

Crochet Lei Scarf

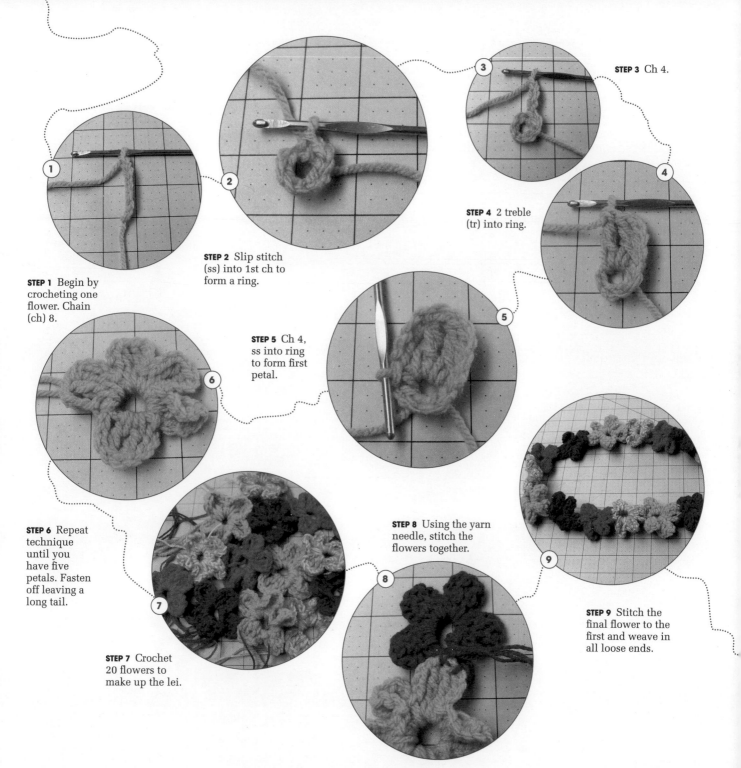

STEP 1 Begin by crocheting one flower. Chain (ch) 8.

STEP 2 Slip stitch (ss) into 1st ch to form a ring.

STEP 3 Ch 4.

STEP 4 2 treble (tr) into ring.

STEP 5 Ch 4, ss into ring to form first petal.

STEP 6 Repeat technique until you have five petals. Fasten off leaving a long tail.

STEP 7 Crochet 20 flowers to make up the lei.

STEP 8 Using the yarn needle, stitch the flowers together.

STEP 9 Stitch the final flower to the first and weave in all loose ends.

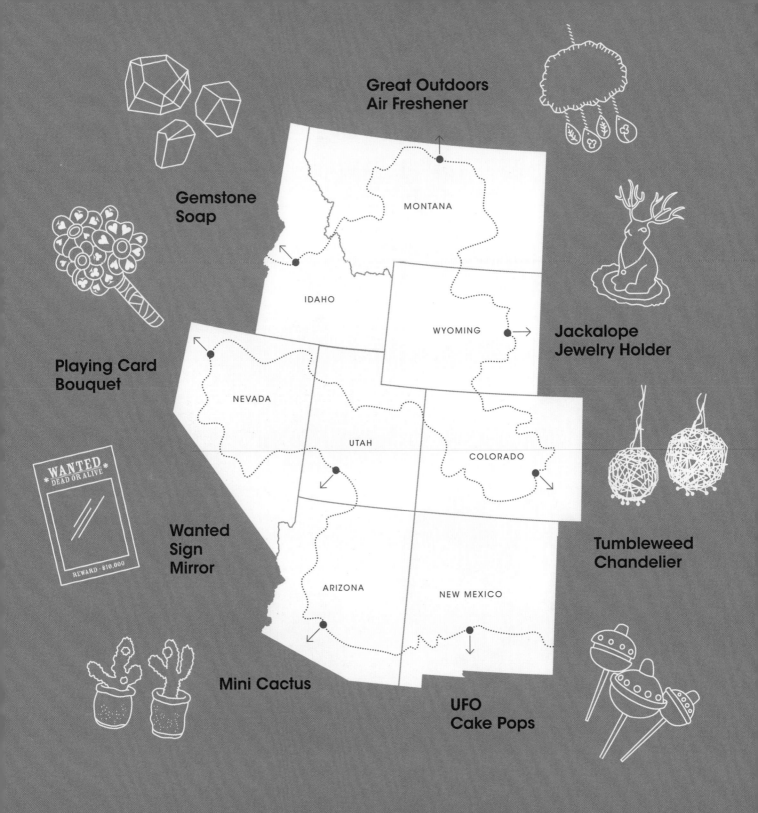

Great Outdoors
Air Freshener

Gemstone
Soap

Jackalope
Jewelry Holder

Playing Card
Bouquet

Tumbleweed
Chandelier

Wanted
Sign
Mirror

Mini Cactus

UFO
Cake Pops

MONTANA

IDAHO

WYOMING

NEVADA

UTAH

COLORADO

ARIZONA

NEW MEXICO

WANTED
* DEAD OR ALIVE *

REWARD - $10,000

Plane parked in the forest.

The world's largest potato, Blackfoot.

The ghost town of Atomic City.

Our room in the world's largest beagle at the Dog Bark Park Inn.

Mammoth skeleton, Grangeville.

Root beer here, Wallace.

Stepping inside a UFO, Wallace.

IDAHO

POST | CARD

With more than 240 different types of mineral, Idaho is known as the Gem State. We found lots of other hidden gems on our drive through it, from amazing parks and odd museums to quirky towns and adorable theme motels.

We began our journey up north in the small town of *Wallace*, where a manhole cover at the intersection of Cedar Street and 6th, in the center of town, was declared the *Center of the Universe* by the town's mayor in 2004. Nearby, you can sit inside a "life-size" UFO and have your photo taken outside the retro *Stardust Motel (410 Pine St.)*. Make sure to try the state fruit, huckleberry, as a milkshake while you're in town, at the *Red Light Garage (302 5th St.)*. Continuing south, we stopped in *Cottonwood* to stay at the *Dog Bark Park Inn (2421 US 95 Business)*, where the friendly owners showed us to our cozy room for the night—inside the world's biggest beagle!

The next day we went on the hunt for *Hell's Canyon*, the deepest gorge in North America. At almost 8,000ft (24,400m) deep, it's deeper than the Grand Canyon, but the weather was too misty for us to get a good view down. Luckily, the sun came out at the *Craters of the Moon National Monument and Preserve* in central Idaho, where ancient lava flows and volcanic formations have created a crazy lunar landscape.

In 1955 the town of *Arco* was the first ever to be lit solely by nuclear power.

In honor of the fact, you can tuck into an Atomic Burger and fried pickles at *Pickle's Place (440 S. Frnt.)*, or take a photo alongside the top of a nuclear submarine.

Spud fans should check out the *Idaho Potato Museum* in *Blackfoot*, where you can find the largest potato in the world, a comprehensive history of the tuber, and pick up some "free 'taters for out-of-staters."

Gemstone Soap

Inspired
by the state's
nickname, gemstone soap
makes the perfect gift
without breaking the bank.

YOU WILL NEED

Melt-and-pour soap
Soap dyes in a variety of colors
Essential oils
Body glitter
Silicone cupcake molds

To make one-color gems:

STEP 1 Cut the melt-and-pour soap into small cubes and place in a microwave-safe bowl. Melt the soap in a microwave, following the manufacturer's instructions.

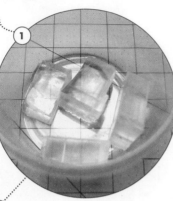

STEP 2 Stir in a few drops of soap dye, essential oil, and body glitter.

STEP 3 Pour the soap into the cupcake molds and leave to set.

STEP 4 Continue this process to make other gem colors.

STEP 5 Pop the soaps out of the molds when they're set.

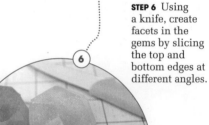

STEP 6 Using a knife, create facets in the gems by slicing the top and bottom edges at different angles.

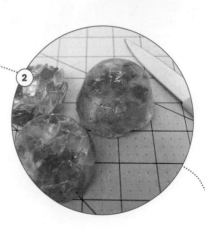

To make multicolored gems:

STEP 1 Chop the scraps from the colored gem soaps into small fragments and place them in the cupcake molds. Melt some more cubes of clear soap in the microwave, pour them over the color fragments, and leave to set.

STEP 2 Facet the bottom edges of the finished soaps, leaving the fragmented top edges uncut.

Giant Montana Tech "M" (for miners) on the hillside, Butte.

Getting advice about forest fires from Smokey the Bear.

Lunch at the Hummingbird Café.

Dinner at The Branch, a train-themed diner in Rexburg.

Our Lady of the Rockies.

Beautiful Montana sunset.

Evel Knievel's grave, Butte.

MONTANA

After leaving Idaho, we headed into Montana. We weren't quite sure what "Big Sky Country" could mean, but as the scenery unfolded into huge, flat expanses with mountain peaks visible all around in the distance, and nothing but pale blue sky in between, we soon understood. Just driving around is breathtaking—except our progress slowed every time we stopped for a photo!

We stopped for lunch at the *Hummingbird Café (605 W. Park St.)* in *Butte*, a copper-mining boom town known as the "richest hill in the USA." With old equipment still in place above mine shafts, it's like stepping into history. Looking down on the city is *Our Lady of the Rockies*, a 90ft (27m)-tall white statue, perched up in the mountains.

Just outside the town is the grave of local daredevil, Evel Knievel, whose famous 1974 failed stunt took place at nearby *Snake River Canyon* (Idaho)—there's an annual celebration held in the town to this day. He still holds the record for surviving the most broken bones in a lifetime (433). One strange piece of history is the *Berkeley Pit*, an old copper mine now heavily contaminated with chemicals, and one of the top tourist attractions in the area!

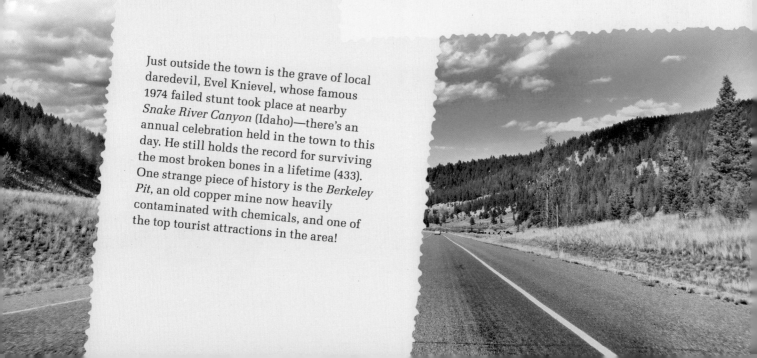

We can't forget how crisp, clean, and fresh the air in Montana was. This all-natural air freshener will bring a hint of the great outdoors to your home.

Before you start this project, gather inspiration by collecting flowers, pine needles, lavender buds, and anything else that smells lovely from your garden.

STEP 1 Press the flowers, leaves, and pine needles overnight in a flower press or between two heavy books.

STEP 2 Draw a simple cloud shape on a piece of paper and cut it out.

Great Outdoors Air Freshener

YOU WILL NEED

Flowers, leaves, and pine needles

Paper

Felt

Essential oils

Stuffing

Contact (sticky-back plastic)

Flower press or heavy books

Needle and thread

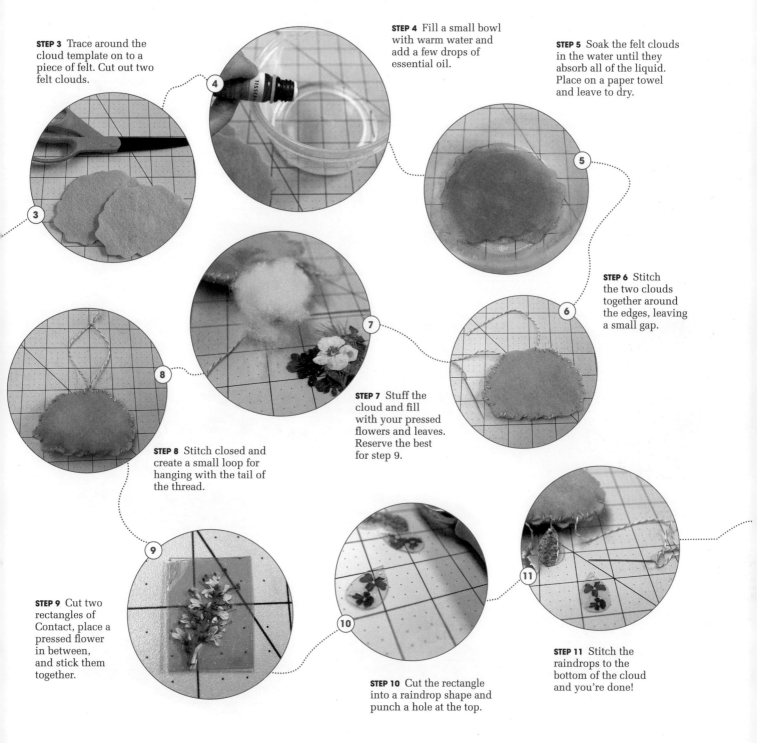

STEP 3 Trace around the cloud template on to a piece of felt. Cut out two felt clouds.

STEP 4 Fill a small bowl with warm water and add a few drops of essential oil.

STEP 5 Soak the felt clouds in the water until they absorb all of the liquid. Place on a paper towel and leave to dry.

STEP 6 Stitch the two clouds together around the edges, leaving a small gap.

STEP 7 Stuff the cloud and fill with your pressed flowers and leaves. Reserve the best for step 9.

STEP 8 Stitch closed and create a small loop for hanging with the tail of the thread.

STEP 9 Cut two rectangles of Contact, place a pressed flower in between, and stick them together.

STEP 10 Cut the rectangle into a raindrop shape and punch a hole at the top.

STEP 11 Stitch the raindrops to the bottom of the cloud and you're done!

The hot water of the Seismograph Pool, Yellowstone National Park.

A raven in Yellowstone.

A steaming hot bubbling pool in Yellowstone.

Old Faithful erupting right on time!

Grazing buffalo, Yellowstone.

Roadside elk holding up the traffic.

WYOMING

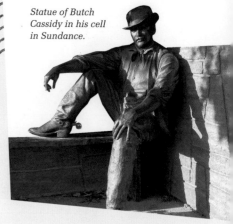

Statue of Butch Cassidy in his cell in Sundance.

A mix of mountains and plains, Wyoming makes for some of the most spectacular scenery in the country. Yellowstone National Park (believed to be the first national park in the world) covers more than 3,000 square miles (almost 8,000 square km) in the west, while the High Plains in the east produce more coal than anywhere else in the country. However, it's the least populous state in America—more people live in Las Vegas than call Wyoming home.

We made our way across the plains to *Cody*, named after William Frederick Cody—better known as Buffalo Bill. We passed vast lakes before coaxing the car up the steep mountains. It's easy to see how the changing landscape has inspired the many myths engraved in the area's folklore.

Fans of the state's "official" mythical creatures should head to *Douglas*, which proclaims itself as home of the "jackalope"—a jackrabbit with antlers. The *World's Largest Jackalope* statue will soon be replaced by an *even bigger* version, and the town celebrates an annual Jackalope Day. Though we weren't able to ride the famous jackalope in *Dubois (W. Rams Horn St.)*, we were able to get our jackalope photo op at *Wall Drug (510 Main St., Wall)* across the border in South Dakota. Clearly, the jackalope knows how to travel!

Yellowstone National Park made an unforgettable first impression as we were greeted by a herd of grazing buffalo. Sitting on top of an active volcano, the park is full of bubbling pools, hot springs, and geysers. We took a seat next to other eager tourists to wait patiently for *Old Faithful* to erupt; luckily, it is true to its name, going off like clockwork every 91 minutes and shooting steam and hot water high in the air. Though we desperately wanted to spot a bear (or even Yogi having a picnic), we were excited to see a herd of elks and a stag holding up the traffic on our way out.

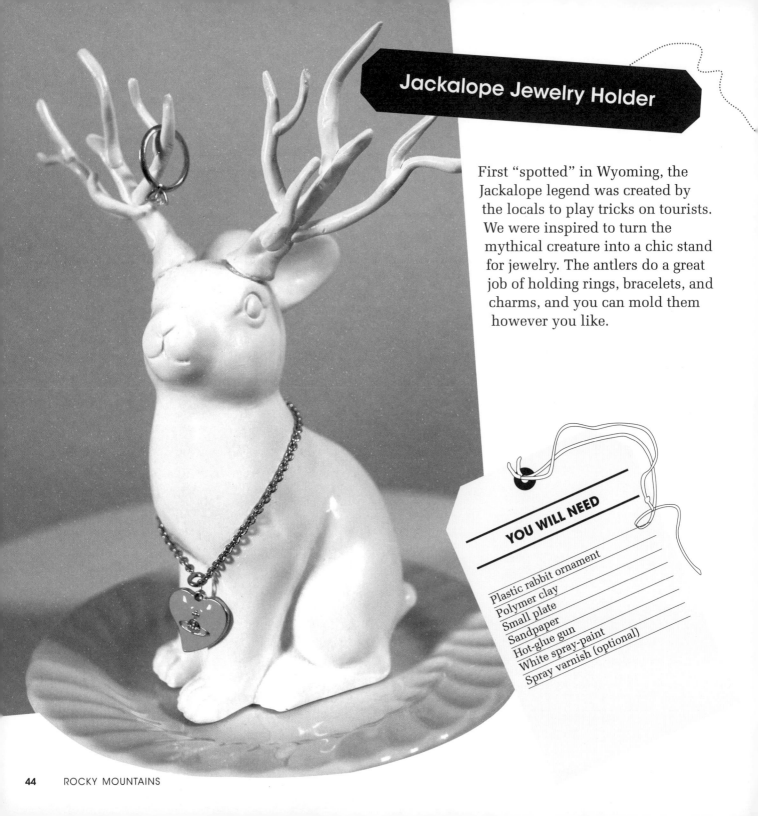

Jackalope Jewelry Holder

First "spotted" in Wyoming, the Jackalope legend was created by the locals to play tricks on tourists. We were inspired to turn the mythical creature into a chic stand for jewelry. The antlers do a great job of holding rings, bracelets, and charms, and you can mold them however you like.

YOU WILL NEED

Plastic rabbit ornament
Polymer clay
Small plate
Sandpaper
Hot-glue gun
White spray-paint
Spray varnish (optional)

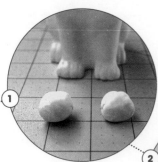

STEP 1 Begin by breaking off two equal-sized balls of polymer clay.

STEP 2 Roll one ball into a cylinder with your fingers. Continue by rolling one end until it tapers out to a long horn. Repeat with the second ball to create a matching horn.

GET CREATIVE!

Invent your own mythical creatures by choosing different plastic animals and sculpting horns, antlers, and other embellishments out of clay.

TIP

Keep an eye out for plastic rabbit decorations around Easter time.

STEP 3 Place the horns on top of the rabbit's head and bend in the shape of antlers.

STEP 4 Repeat the previous steps with smaller balls of clay to build up the antlers, with lots of small branches to hang jewelry on. When you're happy with the design, bake the antlers in the oven (following the manufacturer's instructions) until hard, then leave to cool.

STEP 5 Sand the bottom of each antler, and secure to the rabbit's head using the hot-glue gun.

STEP 6 Spray the jackalope with an even coat of white spray-paint.

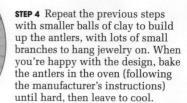

STEP 7 Leave to dry before spraying with a second coat. *Optional: You can apply a coat of spray varnish to give your jackalope extra shine.*

STEP 8 Complete by gluing the jackalope to the plate.

Sunset across the Hoover Dam and Lake Mead.

Hoover Dam Bypass Bridge spanning the Black Canyon.

Welcome to Fabulous Las Vegas!

Downtown Las Vegas.

The Little White Chapel.

Some of the famous weddings held here.

The scale replica of the Eiffel Tower at the Paris Casino.

NEVADA

Although its name means "snowcapped" in Spanish, our first experience of Nevada was the hot desert. Conjuring up romantic images from so many road-trip movies, we imagined we were in a pink Cadillac with our hair blowing in the wind as we made our way toward *Las Vegas*.

After obligatory photos at the famous *Welcome to Las Vegas* sign, and spotting more than a few Elvis impersonators, we headed down the strip. With 62,000 hotel rooms and more than 39 million visitors each year, you don't need us to tell you how to have a good time here. From the 24-story-high fountain jets at the *Bellagio*, to the *MGM* lions, the skyline of *New York-New York*,

or the half-scale Eiffel Tower at the *Paris Casino*, there are bright lights, entertainment, and distraction everywhere. And you don't even need to win big to try another Vegas staple—a marriage license is only $50!

POST CARD

Outside the City of Sin, *Area 51* and the *Extraterrestrial Highway* are popular with tourists hunting UFOs, but we headed south to the *Hoover Dam*. The giant hydroelectric system here uses the Colorado River to generate power, and has created *Lake Mead*, the largest reservoir in the US. The view from the top is breathtaking. Make sure to rub the feet of one of the giant angel statues for good luck—especially if you're heading back to the slot machines.

Playing Card Bouquet

Inspired by the drive-through wedding chapels and casinos of Las Vegas, this beautiful bouquet of diamonds and hearts makes an edgy alternative to flowers—and will stay fresh all year long!

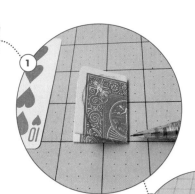

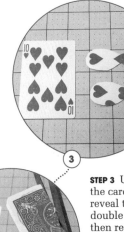

STEP 1 Pick out two cards from the same suit. Fold one in half vertically, then horizontally, then draw the shape of a petal on the front.

STEP 3 Unfold the card to reveal two double petals, then repeat this with the other card.

STEP 2 Cut out the petal with heavy-duty scissors, leaving the bottom edge uncut.

YOU WILL NEED

Playing cards
Eyelets
24-gauge wire
Buttons
Tissue paper
Felt
Ribbon
Heavy-duty scissors
Eyelet punch
Wire cutters

STEP 4 Place the four petals on top of each other and punch a hole through the middle, where the petals meet.

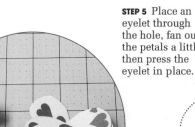

STEP 5 Place an eyelet through the hole, fan out the petals a little, then press the eyelet in place.

STEP 6 Fan out the petals and gently push the petals inward to give the flower some shape.

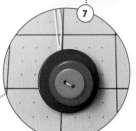

STEP 7 Cut a 24in (60cm) length of wire and fold in half. Select three coordinating small, medium, and large buttons.

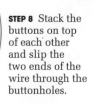

STEP 8 Stack the buttons on top of each other and slip the two ends of the wire through the buttonholes.

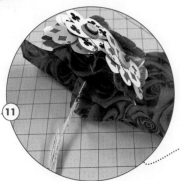

STEP 9 Pass the wire through the eyelet on the flower and slip another small button behind the flower before twisting the wire closed.

STEP 10 Continue making flowers to build up your bouquet, then trim and fold up the tips of the wires to form a smooth end.

STEP 11 Arrange some decorative tissue paper around the top of the bouquet and tape in place.

STEP 12 Wrap a square of felt around the wire stalk.

STEP 13 Tie some ribbon around the stalk and your bouquet is complete!

Balancing Rock, Arches National Park.

A home painted as a replica of the house in Pixar's film Up.

The landscape on Route 6 in Carbon County.

The ghost town of Cody, Utah.

Being welcomed to Arches National Park by a bighorn sheep!

The waterfall at the Mormon Conference Center.

Making shadows under the arches.

POST | CARD

Driving through the desert and canyons of Utah feels so familiar—likely from all the Western movies filmed here. We thought our eyes were playing tricks on us when a conelike dust shape appeared to blow across the desert, but later found out these are mini-tornadoes, known as "dust devils," and are really fun to look out for.

In the southeast of the state, the *Arches National Park* contains incredible rock sculptures, carved by thousands of years of erosion. From skyscraper shapes, to balancing rocks, and the iconic freestanding arches, we were surrounded by some of the most out-of-this-world scenery we've ever seen.

The ghost town of *Cisco* was once a water-refilling station for steam locomotives. Nowadays, with around five residents, it's a collection of fallen-down buildings, abandoned homes, and an eerie, enchanting atmosphere.

Returning to civilization, we made our way toward the capital, *Salt Lake City*. Much saltier than seawater, and very shallow, the *Great Salt Lake* has a strange presence, with lines of salt deposits along its banks. The city was founded by Brigham Young, who started the Mormon Church here.

Although you're not able to visit the *Salt Lake Temple* without an invitation, there are regular tours of the *Tabernacle* and shiny new *Conference Center*, where you can learn more about the faith. Visible across the city, the twin peaks of *Mount Olympus* were host to the Winter Olympics in 2002.

Just like Utah-born Butch Cassidy, if you've gone 'n' done it, the sheriff'll be wantin' to speak to you! Make sure your mugshot is picture-perfect with this mirror.

Wanted Sign Mirror

YOU WILL NEED

Sticker paper
Paper
Mirror
Masking tape
Craft knife
Etching spray

WANTED

DEAD OR ALIVE

REWARD - $10,000

STEP 1 Print out your lettering design on to sticker paper.

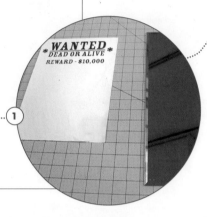

STEP 2 Tape a piece of paper down in the center of the mirror. This will be the main clean area of the mirror, so choose the size you'd like this to be.

STEP 3 Position the lettering on the mirror and Blu-tack it in place.

STEP 4 Use the craft knife to cut out each of the letters carefully.

STEP 5 Peel the back off each of the letters and stick in place on the mirror, using the remaining outline as a guide.

GET CREATIVE:

Personalize your mirror by changing the reason for the warrant.

STEP 6 Remove the paper outline and spray the mirror with etching spray.

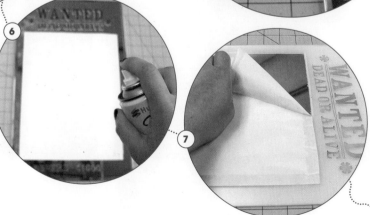

STEP 7 Leave to dry before removing the center paper and sticker letters. You can tidy up any messy areas by scratching off the excess etching spray.

Vintage cars at the Wigwam Motel, Flagstaff.

Retro cars along Route 66 in Seligman.

Racoons at Bearizona.

Route 66 Grill, Ask Fork.

The Grand Canyon.

Souvenirs from the Roadkill Café, Seligman.

Lost in Seligman?
This sign will point you the right way!

ARIZONA

Arizona is home to one of America's most iconic landmarks, the *Grand Canyon*. We took in the wonders of its vast landscape, with *huge* depths and craggy rocks as far as we could see. Despite the huge and perilous cliff faces, the biggest danger in the canyon is the rock squirrel, which is known to bite visitors frequently!

Back on the road, we continued along Route 66. The stretch between *Seligman* and *Kingman* is part of the longest remaining stretch of the famous road, and each small town along the way was filled with retro cars, stores, diners, and more than one Elvis mannequin. The new Interstate Highway now bypasses all of these towns, leaving tumbleweeds to drift across the old road.

We didn't expect to encounter any bears in the middle of the desert until we spotted signs for *Bearizona*, a drive-through safari park where you can get up close and personal to black bears and other wildlife from the safety of your car. The mission of the park is to promote conservation, and we loved seeing bear cubs playing in their natural environment. The park's picturesque trails also make this the ideal place to stretch your legs on a long road trip.

Next, we headed south through the desert to the famous red rocks and hippie community of *Sedona*. We stopped for dinner at the UFO- and alien-themed *Red Planet Diner (1655 Arizona 89A)*, with a panoramic view over the rocks, and rested our heads for the night at the *Wigwam Motel (811 W. Hopi Dr.)* in Holbrook. This motel was one of the iconic stop-off points for tourists traveling Route 66. Don't worry about getting cold—the teepees are made from solid concrete!

Our final stop in Arizona was the *Petrified Forest*, where wood from 225 million years ago has fossilized into colorful shapes scattered across the land.

Mini Cactus

Want to bring a piece of the desert into your home? A needle-felted cactus is the perfect project for creating your very own oasis, and you don't even have to water it!

YOU WILL NEED

Brown polymer clay
Terra-cotta polymer clay
Green wire
Green wool roving
Pink wool roving
Mini rolling pin
Craft knife
Awl
Wire cutters
Felting needle and mat

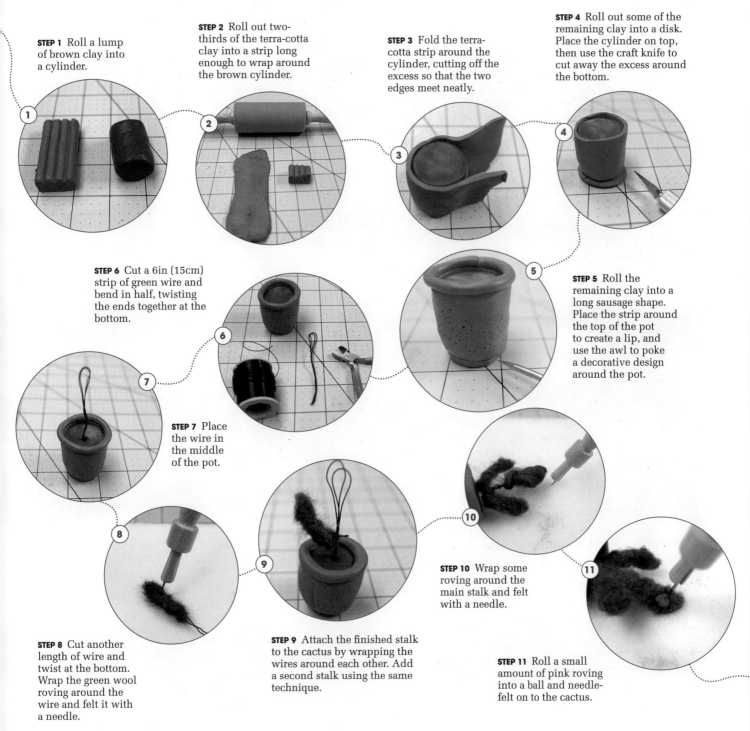

STEP 1 Roll a lump of brown clay into a cylinder.

STEP 2 Roll out two-thirds of the terra-cotta clay into a strip long enough to wrap around the brown cylinder.

STEP 3 Fold the terra-cotta strip around the cylinder, cutting off the excess so that the two edges meet neatly.

STEP 4 Roll out some of the remaining clay into a disk. Place the cylinder on top, then use the craft knife to cut away the excess around the bottom.

STEP 5 Roll the remaining clay into a long sausage shape. Place the strip around the top of the pot to create a lip, and use the awl to poke a decorative design around the pot.

STEP 6 Cut a 6in (15cm) strip of green wire and bend in half, twisting the ends together at the bottom.

STEP 7 Place the wire in the middle of the pot.

STEP 8 Cut another length of wire and twist at the bottom. Wrap the green wool roving around the wire and felt it with a needle.

STEP 9 Attach the finished stalk to the cactus by wrapping the wires around each other. Add a second stalk using the same technique.

STEP 10 Wrap some roving around the main stalk and felt with a needle.

STEP 11 Roll a small amount of pink roving into a ball and needle-felt on to the cactus.

Mountain goats on Mount Evans.

Bear made of nails, Aspen.

Statue at Mesa Verde.

Taking a ride on the Georgetown Loop Railroad.

Exploring the ancient dwellings of Mesa Verde.

The Historic Argo Gold Mine, Idaho Springs.

Waffles at Lucile's, Boulder.

ARGO
GOLD MINE & MILL

COLORADO

"Welcome to Colorful Colorado" boasts the state sign, and crossing the border into the state, it's easy to see why. Our first stop was the college town of *Boulder*. We had breakfast at *Lucile's (2124 14th St.)* and warmed up with flowering pots of tea at *Dushanbe Tea House (1770 13th St.)* before heading into the mountains, where we caught the *Georgetown Loop Railroad* through the mountains to *Silver Plume*, an old ghost town. The twists and turns mean the train takes 4 miles (6.5km) of track to connect two towns only 2 miles (3.2km) apart.

Up in the Rocky Mountains, the resort of *Aspen* is picturesque and posh, with boutiques and fancy restaurants catering to celebrities on skiing vacations. We took the *Top of the Rockies* road, which twists and hairpins across the Continental Divide through *Independence Pass*, leading to the highest city in the country, *Leadville*, at more than 10,000ft (3,000m). A silver-mining boom once made this Colorado's second biggest city, but now the abandoned mines and unusual history make for a great visit.

For road trippers, *Mount Evans* is the perfect way to tackle a peak without leaving the car. It's the highest paved road in the US, and we reached the top as mountain goats looked on. Be careful not to stay too long at the top—at 14,000 ft (4,300m), altitude sickness can kick in!

POST | CARD

We loved our time in *Denver*. Jelly *(1700 E. Evans Ave.)* serves great brunch amid cereal-box decor, a giant bear peering into the *Convention Center* provides a great photo op, and the grand *Union Station* is a downtown landmark.

City Park is great for a view of downtown Denver, and it's near the hip *Colfax* neighborhood. We spent the evening at the *88 Drive-In Theatre*, where a triple feature in the rain drained our car battery. Luckily, they had booster cables on hand.

Driving in the southwest of the state, we passed cowboys herding dozens of cows on our way to *Mesa Verde*. The cliff dwellings here are more than 1,000 years old, with hundreds of rooms to explore.

Out in the snow at the Continental Divide.

INDEPENDENCE PASS
ELEVATION 12,095 FEET
CONTINENTAL DIVIDE

Tumbleweed Chandelier

YOU WILL NEED:

Balloon
PVA glue
Twine
Fairy lights

Inspired
by the tumbleweeds
blowing through the ghost town of
Silver Plume, this rustic chandelier
adds a sparkle to any room.

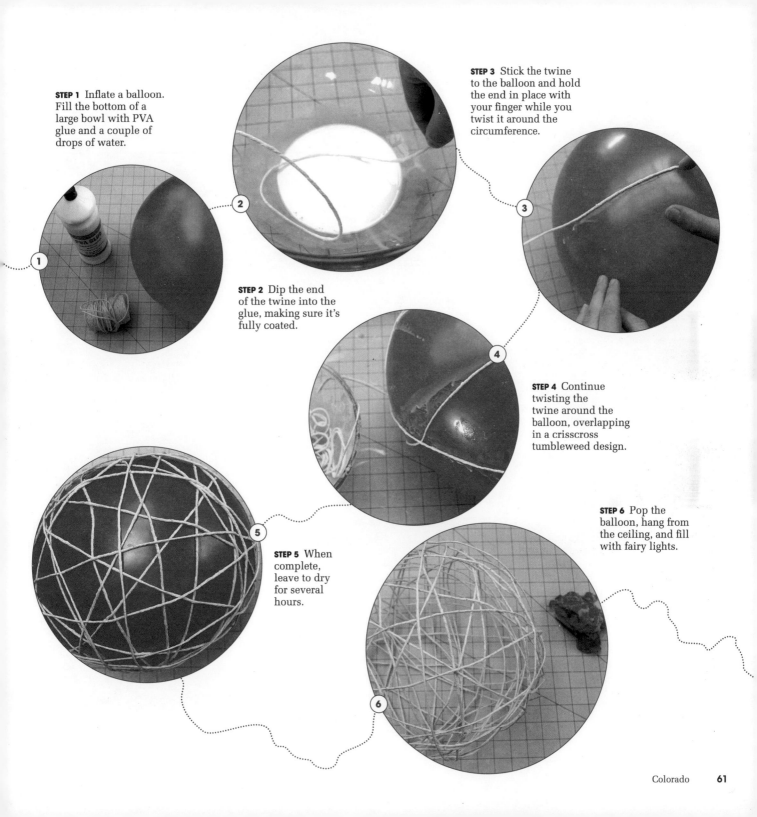

STEP 1 Inflate a balloon. Fill the bottom of a large bowl with PVA glue and a couple of drops of water.

STEP 2 Dip the end of the twine into the glue, making sure it's fully coated.

STEP 3 Stick the twine to the balloon and hold the end in place with your finger while you twist it around the circumference.

STEP 4 Continue twisting the twine around the balloon, overlapping in a crisscross tumbleweed design.

STEP 5 When complete, leave to dry for several hours.

STEP 6 Pop the balloon, hang from the ceiling, and fill with fairy lights.

Keep an eye out for odd-shaped rocks in the desert.

The haunted Double Eagle Restaurant, Mesilla.

Meeting the aliens in Roswell.

The Oldest House in America, Santa Fe.

Santa Fe turquoise and terra-cotta ornaments.

Becoming an alien, Roswell.

Checking in to the Silver Saddle Motel, Santa Fe.

New Mexico

502 WEST
Los Alamos
EXIT ↓ ONLY

As we headed east, the rocks and cliffs of Arizona transformed into the flat desert of New Mexico. There are 22 Native American tribes here, each with their own government and traditions, and their influence on art and design is everywhere.

At the *Four Corners*, we stood on the state's border with Colorado, Arizona, and Utah, simultaneously! Farther west, the *Los Alamos National Laboratory* was top secret during World War II, as it was home to the scientists who created the first atomic bombs. Nowadays it's a huge museum and research center, with teams working on HIV vaccination and renewable energy.

The state capital, *Santa Fe*, is the second oldest city in the whole country; with strict building regulations on height and materials, it is full of orange and beige adobe. We stayed at the *Silver Saddle Motel (2810 Cerrillos Road)*, which was full of Western kitsch, before exploring the historic streets and stumbling across the *Oldest House in America (215 E. De Vargas St.)*.

The small town of *Roswell* is best known for a supposed 1947 UFO landing, and the *International UFO Museum and Research Center* explores this controversial story. Everything from the streetlights and storefronts have been alien-ed up a little, too. Our own UFO story is typical of most. After spotting a shiny *something* glistening in the sky, we reached for our camera. But, just like that, it had disappeared again. Of course, this was before we got the all-important picture. Dang!

All along the road east to Texas we passed beautiful ironwork silhouettes from *Poor Boys Metal Art (305 E. Bdwy., Tatum)*. Then we hit the south of the state, with its strong Spanish and Mexican influences. We loved the town of *Las Cruces* on the Rio Grande, and stopped at the *Double Eagle Restaurant (2355 Calle De Guadalupe)* in *Mesilla*, where the ghosts of two teenage lovers are said to inhabit the halls.

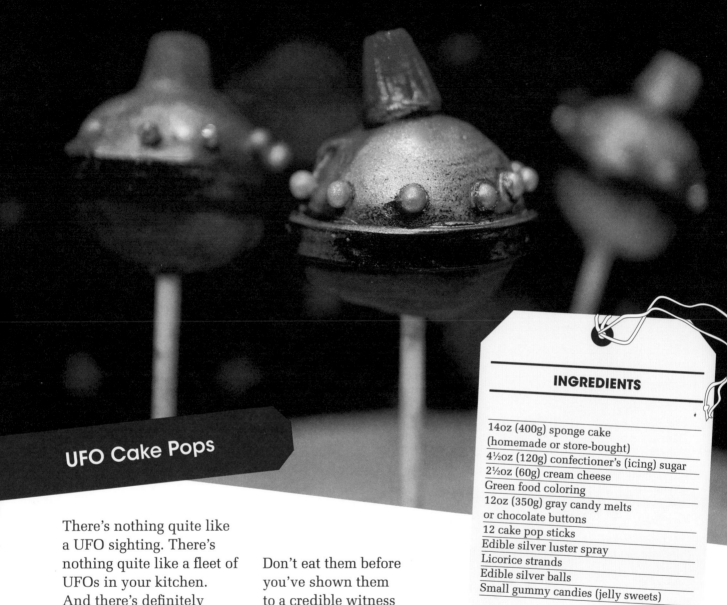

UFO Cake Pops

There's nothing quite like a UFO sighting. There's nothing quite like a fleet of UFOs in your kitchen. And there's definitely nothing like enjoying a classic cake pop.

Don't eat them before you've shown them to a credible witness though—nobody'll believe you once they're gone!

INGREDIENTS

14oz (400g) sponge cake (homemade or store-bought)

4½oz (120g) confectioner's (icing) sugar

2½oz (60g) cream cheese

Green food coloring

12oz (350g) gray candy melts or chocolate buttons

12 cake pop sticks

Edible silver luster spray

Licorice strands

Edible silver balls

Small gummy candies (jelly sweets)

Makes 12

STEP 1 Break the sponge cake into pieces and place in a blender.

STEP 2 Add the confectioner's sugar, cream cheese, and green food coloring and blitz until you have a smooth consistency.

STEP 3 Roll the dough into 12 small balls and chill in the refrigerator for several hours.

STEP 4 Prepare your toppings—you'll need 12 strips of licorice, 12 gummy candies, silver luster spray, and a bowl of edible silver balls.

TIP:

If you're struggling to get the candy melt runny enough, stir in a couple of drops of vegetable oil.

STEP 5 Melt the candy melts in a microwave-safe bowl until silky and runny.

STEP 6 Dip the ends of the cake pop sticks into the candy melt, then stick them into the cake balls.

STEP 7 One by one, dip the cake balls into the candy melt, making sure they are evenly coated, then place them in a cake pop stand.

STEP 8 Spray each cake pop with silver luster dust.

STEP 9 While the candy melt is still wet, wrap the licorice around each cake pop, decorate with silver balls, and place a gummy candy on top. Leave to set.

New Mexico   **65**

Origami
Sunflower Clock

Roll-up
Shopping Tote

Postcard
Travel Pillow

Pie Shakes

Cornhusk
to Popcorn
Plushie

Bottle Cap Ring

Ruby Red
Shoes

Old Shack
Bird Box

Route 66
Vintage Tee

South Dakota

NORTH DAKOTA

MINNESOTA

SOUTH DAKOTA

IOWA

NEBRASKA

KANSAS

MISSOURI

OKLAHOMA

ARKANSAS

KEEP OUT

US 66

The landscape was so flat!

Downtown Fargo.

Finding some yarn bombing.

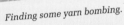

Lunch at Green Market.

Steamboats on the Red River plaque, Fargo.

Fargo Theatre.

Craft inspiration: A clock in Fargo.

NORTH DAKOTA

North Dakota was the state where we realized we *really* wanted to see all the states. Our drive back from Minneapolis to Omaha would be covering the same ground ... unless we took a "slight" detour via *Fargo!* It's home to *New Salem's* fiberglass *Salem Sue* (the world's largest Holstein cow), and the *Geographical Center of North America* in *Rugby.*

The first thing we noticed was how flat the landscape was—nothing but grasslands as far as the eye could see. If you find yourself getting a little bored by the scenery, take a detour down the *Enchanted Highway* in *Regent*, where a retired school teacher has created a series of giant roadside sculptures.

We made our way to *Fargo*, a city we'd learned about from the Coen Brothers' movie of the same name, but, unlike the harsh winter landscape in the film, it was a warm summer's day when we visited. The flowers were in full bloom, making the bouquet-lined streets look so pretty. We took a walk down the *Fargo Walk of Fame*, outside the *Fargo-Moorhead Convention and Visitor's Bureau (2001 44th St. S.)*, where you can find the famous wood-chipper from the movie.

Agriculture is big business in North Dakota, and one of the top crops is the sunflower, with the state producing over 40 percent of the nation's supply. Of course, *lots* of bees are needed to pollinate the flowers, so the state is a top honey producer as well!

YOU WILL NEED

Yellow origami paper
Brown card
Clock kit
Paper clips
Craft knife
Hot-glue gun

We loved seeing sunflowers on our trip, and this clock will bring a little sunshine into your home.

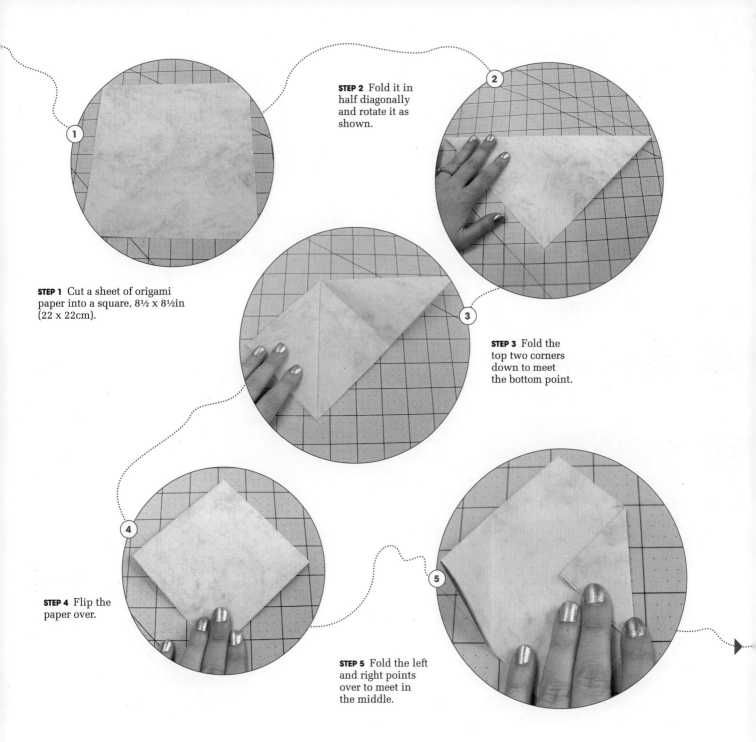

STEP 1 Cut a sheet of origami paper into a square, 8½ x 8½in (22 x 22cm).

STEP 2 Fold it in half diagonally and rotate it as shown.

STEP 3 Fold the top two corners down to meet the bottom point.

STEP 4 Flip the paper over.

STEP 5 Fold the left and right points over to meet in the middle.

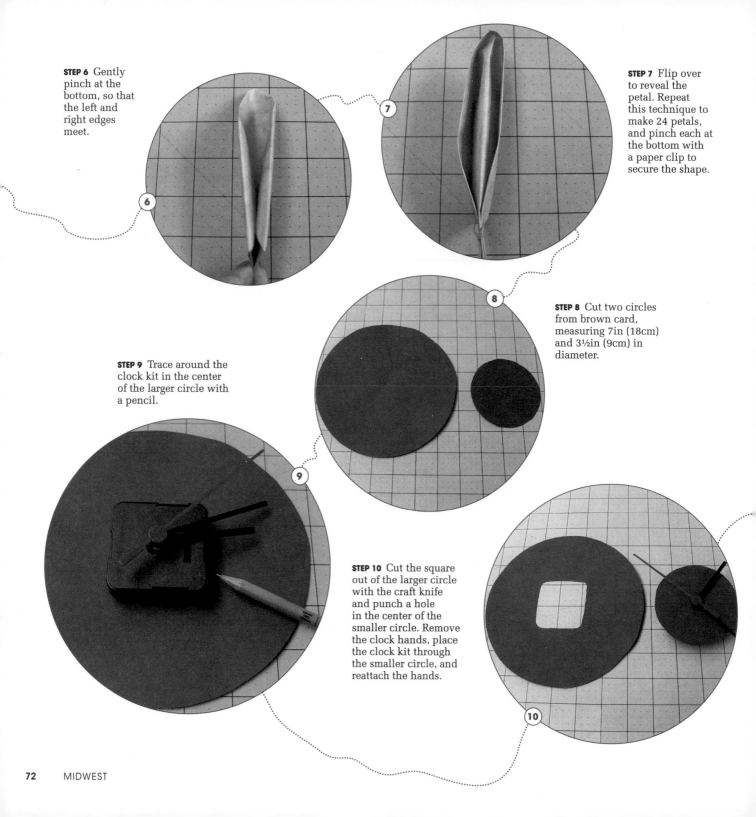

STEP 6 Gently pinch at the bottom, so that the left and right edges meet.

STEP 7 Flip over to reveal the petal. Repeat this technique to make 24 petals, and pinch each at the bottom with a paper clip to secure the shape.

STEP 8 Cut two circles from brown card, measuring 7in (18cm) and 3½in (9cm) in diameter.

STEP 9 Trace around the clock kit in the center of the larger circle with a pencil.

STEP 10 Cut the square out of the larger circle with the craft knife and punch a hole in the center of the smaller circle. Remove the clock hands, place the clock kit through the smaller circle, and reattach the hands.

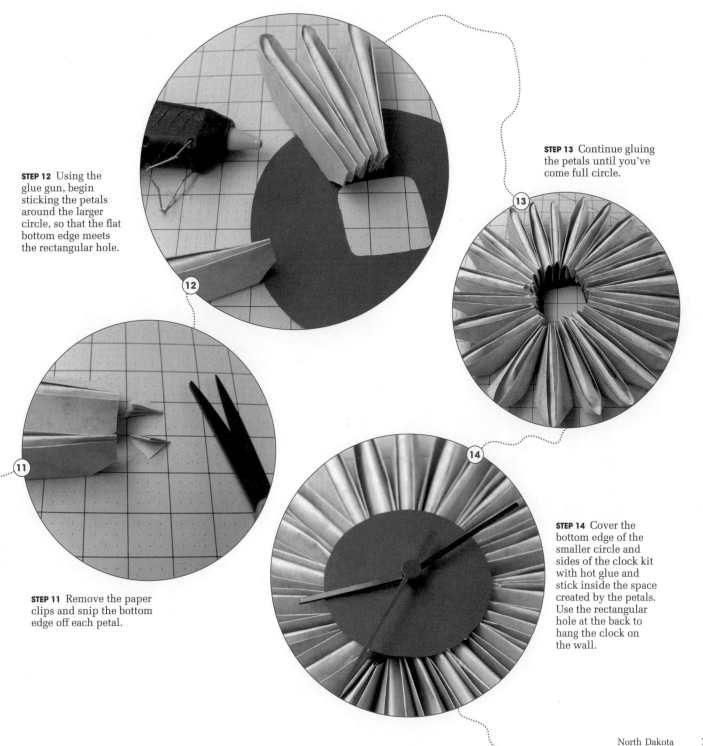

STEP 12 Using the glue gun, begin sticking the petals around the larger circle, so that the flat bottom edge meets the rectangular hole.

STEP 13 Continue gluing the petals until you've come full circle.

STEP 11 Remove the paper clips and snip the bottom edge off each petal.

STEP 14 Cover the bottom edge of the smaller circle and sides of the clock kit with hot glue and stick inside the space created by the petals. Use the rectangular hole at the back to hang the clock on the wall.

Washington, Jefferson, Roosevelt, and Lincoln at Mount Rushmore.

Waterfall on the Big Sioux River, Sioux Falls.

Sizing up to a giant prairie dog at Prairie Dog Town.

Murals made of corn kernels on the side of the Mitchell Corn Palace.

One of many billboards advertising Wall Drug Store in Wall.

Human and T-rex sculpture, Murdo.

A real prairie dog at Prairie Dog Town.

SOUTH DAKOTA

South Dakota is covered in prairies and grasslands, but what this flat landscape lacks, the locals have more than made up for with man-made landmarks and offbeat tourist attractions. Our first stop was *Sioux Falls*, where we took in the impressive sight of the town's namesake waterfalls before tucking into a deep-fried Twinkie at the *Phillips Avenue Diner (121 S. Phillips Ave.)*. A short drive along the highway, we stopped off in *Mitchell* to see the world's only *Corn Palace (601 N. Main St.)*, an arena building decorated and entirely covered in corn, with designs changing every year.

Covering a gigantic 240,000 acres (97,000 hectares), the *Badlands National Park* breaks up the flat landscape with towering rock peaks, layered with color. You wouldn't expect to see much living in such a harsh environment, but if you look closely you might be able to spot a little prairie dog popping out of a hole in the ground. We got to meet these adorable critters at the *Ranch Store (Hwy. 240 Loop Rd.)* in *Cactus Flat*, where you can pose with a giant prairie dog or pick up some food to feed them out in the yard.

As we made our way along the highway, we began to notice more and more billboards for somewhere called *Wall Drug*, so by the time we reached the remote town of *Wall* we couldn't resist stopping off. Drawing two million tourists a year, this drugstore is the perfect place to pick up souvenirs and pose for photos. Our final stop was America's most iconic man-made landmark, *Mount Rushmore*. It's not easy to get up close, though, so the scale of the 60ft (18m)-tall faces was a little lost on us!

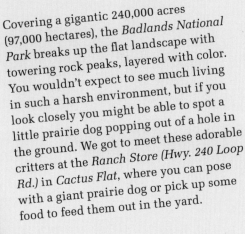

Cool off with a peanut butter milkshake in Sioux Falls.

Postcard Travel Pillow

We came back from our visit to South Dakota with a lot of pictures that look straight off a postcard.

Turn a favorite vacation snap into a travel pillow that will be the envy of your fellow passengers.

South Dakota

Wish you were here...

YOU WILL NEED:

Photo
Image-editing software
Computer and printer
Transfer paper
Cotton fabric
Stuffing
Sewing machine
Needle and thread

Design your postcard:

Pick a vacation photo that you think will look good as a postcard and open it in any image-editing software. Turn the image sepia for a vintage feel, and add a white border around the outside to give it the postcard look. Add some text, such as the place name or "Wish you were here," and design the back of your postcard with lines and a scan of a stamp.

Important—you must now mirror both sides of your design!

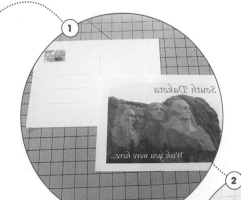

STEP 1 Print the front and back of the design on to transfer paper.

STEP 2 Iron the design on to two rectangles of cotton fabric.

STEP 3 Carefully peel the transfer paper from the fabric to reveal the design and cut around the outline, leaving a ⅝in (1.5cm) seam allowance.

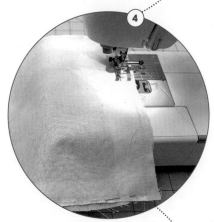

STEP 4 Right sides together, sew around the edges of the postcard, leaving a small gap.

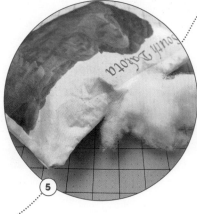

STEP 5 Turn the pillow right side out and stuff it.

STEP 6 Hand-stitch the small gap closed.

Dome above the world's largest indoor desert, Henry Doorly Zoo.

Mural in downtown Omaha.

Cat's looking forward to the Good Life!

Neon ice-cream sign at Ted & Wally's, Omaha.

Fairy-lit horse and cart rides around the Old Market, Omaha.

The world's largest ball of stamps, Boys Town.

Dale Chihuly, Inside and Out, 2000, Joslyn Art Museum, Omaha.

NeBraska

"The Good Life" is a pretty accurate description of our time in Nebraska—the welcoming, friendly, and laid-back attitude of this state's inhabitants made us feel at home straight away.

We stopped off in *North Platte*, where 10,000 railroad cars pass through the largest rail yard in the world. The *Golden Spike Tower* gave us an amazing view over the yard, before we headed east to the state capital, *Lincoln*. There are museums dedicated to tractors, telephones, and even roller-skating, but the biggest draw for many visitors is to watch the *Huskers* play football at the gigantic *Memorial Stadium*. When it's at capacity, it holds more people than Nebraska's third largest city!

The *Old Market* in downtown *Omaha* is full of vintage stores and restaurants. Our first discovery was *Hollywood Candy (1209 Jackson St.)*, an antique lover and candy addict's paradise. If your sugar craving hasn't been satisfied, *Ted & Wally's (1120 Jackson St.)* churn unique flavors of ice cream on vintage machines in an old gas station. If music is your thing, the *Slowdown (729 N. 14th St.)* bar and *Saddle Creek Store (721 N. 14th St.)* in north downtown are renowned indie hotspots.

At *Omaha's Henry Doorly Zoo (3701 S. 10th St.)* we explored the rainforest and visited an indoor swamp before taking the Skyfari high over some snoozing baby giraffes! For more *local* wildlife, the *Alpine Inn (10405 Calhoun Rd.)* has huge windows looking out over racoons, who feast on fried chicken leftovers. The oldest café in the city, *Lisa's Radial (817 N. 40th St.)*, serves a great breakfast, but we couldn't get enough of *Blue Sushi's (416 S. 12th St.)* happy hour.

Sign from the Overland train, which ran from Omaha to San Francisco, Durham Museum.

Cornhusk to Popcorn Plushie

They don't call it the cornhusker state for nothing—the roads are lined with ear after ear. This plushie will remind you of one of corn's best uses.

YOU WILL NEED

Yellow light worsted (DK) yarn
White light worsted (DK) yarn
Red light worsted (DK) yarn
Green light worsted (DK) yarn
2 small black beads
Black embroidery floss
G-6 (4mm) crochet hook
Yarn needle
Embroidery needle

This project uses US terminology. For a table of UK terms, please see page 240.

① Crochet the popcorn:

Round 1: Using yellow yarn, chain (ch) 2, 4 single crochet (sc) in second ch from hook. (4 sts) (Do not slip stitch to join into a ring; you will be working in a spiral.)
Round 2: 2 sc in each sc around. (8 sts)
Round 3: 2 sc in next 4 sc, sc to end. (12 sts)
Round 4: 2 sc in next 4 sc, sc to end. (16 sts)
Round 5: 2 sc in next 4 sc, sc to end. (20 sts)
Round 6: 2 sc in next 4 sc, sc to end. (24 sts)

Rounds 7–22: Sc in each sc.
Round 23: Sc2tog 4 times, sc to end. (20 sts)
Rounds 24–27: Sc in each sc.
Round 28: Sc2tog 4 times, sc to end. (16 sts)
Rounds 29–32: Sc in each sc.
Round 33: Sc2tog 4 times, sc to end. (12 sts)
Rounds 34–37: Sc in each sc.
Fasten off leaving a long tail.

(2) Crochet the striped box:

Row 1: Using white yarn, ch 9, sc in 2nd ch from hook, sc into each ch across. (8 sts)

Rows 2–4: Ch 1, turn, sc into each sc.

Rows 5–9: Using red yarn, ch 1, turn, sc into each sc.

Rows 10–14: Using white yarn, ch 1, turn, sc into each sc.

Rows 15–19: Using red yarn, ch 1, turn, sc into each sc.

Rows 20–24: Using white yarn, ch 1, turn, sc into each sc.

Rows 25–29: Using red yarn, ch 1, turn, sc into each sc.

Rows 30–34: Using white yarn, ch 1, turn, sc into each sc.

Rows 35–39: Using red yarn, ch 1, turn, sc into each sc.

Rows 40–44: Using white yarn, ch 1, turn, sc into each sc.

Rows 45–49: Using red yarn, ch 1, turn, sc into each sc., dc into each dc across.

Rows 50–54: Using white yarn, ch 1, turn, sc into each sc.

Rows 54–59: Using red yarn, ch 1, turn, sc into each sc. Fasten off.

Using white yarn, crochet a rim along the top of the striped box:

Row 1: Sc evenly along the edge. (60 sts)

Row 2: Ch 1, turn, sc in each sc across. Fasten off, leaving a long tail.

(3) Crochet the leaves (make 3):

Row 1: Using green yarn, ch 13, sc in 2nd ch from hook, sc into each ch to end. (12 sts)

Rows 2–3: Ch 1, turn, sc to end of row.

Row 4: Ch 1, turn, sc2tog, sc into next 8 sc, sc2tog. (10 sts)

Rows 5–7: Ch 1, turn, sc to end of row.

Row 8: Ch 1, turn, sc2tog, sc into next 6 sc, sc2tog. (8 sts)

Rows 9–11: Ch 1, turn, sc to end of row.

Row 12: Ch 1, turn, sc2tog, sc into next 4 sc, sc2tog. (6 sts)

Rows 13–15: Ch 1, turn, sc to end of row.

Row 16: Ch 1, turn, sc2tog, sc into next 2 sc, sc2tog. (4 sts)

Rows 17–19: Ch 1, turn, sc to end of row.

Row 20: Ch 1, turn, sc2tog twice. (2 sts)

Row 21: Ch 1, turn, sc2tog. (1 st) Fasten off, leaving a long tail.

Note: Our popcorn piece measured 3⅛ x 3⅜in (8 x 8.5cm), the leaves were 2in (5cm) wide at the bottom and 3⅜in (8.5cm) tall, and the box piece was 7⅛ x 2⅜in (18 x 6cm).

Making up:

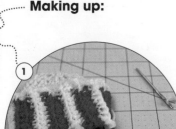

STEP 1 Place the corn inside the popcorn box and, using the yellow tail of the corn, stitch together along the bottom edge. Weave in the loose ends.

STEP 2 Using the long white tail of the popcorn box, stitch the box closed.

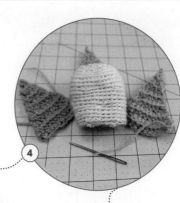

STEP 3 Stitch the top of the popcorn box to the corn with one little stitch, fasten off, and weave in loose ends.

STEP 4 Turn the popcorn box inside out and using the green tails, stitch the three leaves to the bottom edge of the corn. Fasten off and weave in all loose ends.

STEP 5 Stitch a small mouth with black embroidery floss and two black beads for eyes on to the front of the corn.

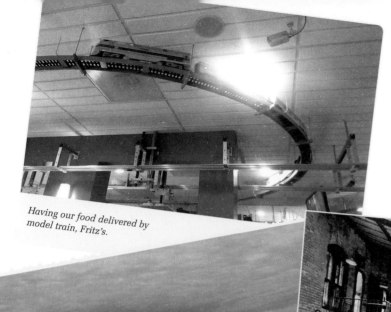

Having our food delivered by model train, Fritz's.

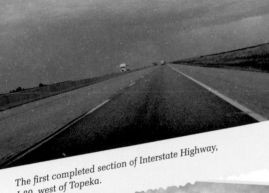

Cute chipmunk in Kansas City.

The first completed section of Interstate Highway, I-80, west of Topeka.

The brick buildings of Wichita.

In 1874, grasshoppers invaded Kansas. We saw one!

The Kansas Turnpike, which once ended at a field on the Oklahoma state line.

At Fritz's, looking forward to dinner after a long day!

KANSAS

Kansas is infamous for its weather—the flat landscape and hot, humid summers create the perfect conditions for tornadoes. Right in the middle of Tornado Alley we felt a knot in our stomachs as the sky became dark. We'd experienced our first "tornado warning" a few weeks earlier in *Omaha*, when we looked out of the window to see an ominous-looking cloud coming closer and closer. It was only seconds after asking "Does that look like a tornado to you?" that sirens started droning, the sky turned black, and the temperature dropped. Luckily it was just a rain cloud this time, and the sun soon started shining as we made our way to *Wichita*.

Wichita is the largest city in Kansas, and home to the very first Pizza Hut. Crafters will love *Mrs. O'Leary's (25 N. Rock Island St.)*, a quirky little supply store that will make you feel like you're in Grandma's house. We were also recommended *Odd Balls Yarn Shop (2120 N. Woodlawn, Suite 324)* and *The Onion Tree (120 N. Hillside)*.

Strolling through the beautiful cobbled streets of the Old Town made me wish I had been wearing a pair of Dorothy's ruby red shoes. On that note, *Wizard of Oz* fans will definitely want to check out *Dorothy's House and Land of Oz (567 E. Cedar St.)* in *Liberal*, northern Kansas.

It was then time to get back on the road and drive northeast to *Kansas City*, a city split in two by the state line with Missouri. We stopped for dinner at *Fritz's Railroad Restaurant (13803 W. 63rd St., Shawnee)*, a train-themed fast-food restaurant chain, with several outlets around the city. A toy train set circled the restaurant and we sat in a booth, ordered our meal via a phone on the table, and watched in amazement as our food was delivered by a train lowering a tray from the ceiling.

These shoes are so sparkly that you'll feel like you're not in Kansas any more!

Ruby Red Shoes

STEP 1 Fill a small pot with Mod Podge and mix in a large amount of glitter.

STEP 2 Using the foam brush, paint the outside of the shoes with one thick coat and leave to dry.

STEP 3 Mix up a second batch of glittery glue and paint the shoes with a second coat, making sure that you've not missed any patches. Leave the shoes to dry completely.

STEP 4 Stitch sparkly red trim around the top edge of each shoe.

STEP 5 Finish by stitching a pretty bow with a button in the middle on to each shoe.

Mailboxes on Route 66.

Bricktown in Oklahoma City.

Cupcake toothpaste at Pinkitzel.

The American Banjo Museum, Oklahoma City.

Stopping for a drink at Pops' giant soda bottle sculpture.

Myriad Botanical Gardens, Oklahoma City.

Bricktown water tower.

OKLAHOMA

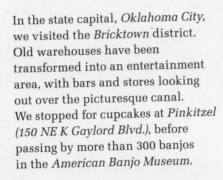

Though you might only be familiar with the musical, Oklahoma has a *lot* more to offer than wind sweeping down the plain!

In the state capital, *Oklahoma City*, we visited the *Bricktown* district. Old warehouses have been transformed into an entertainment area, with bars and stores looking out over the picturesque canal. We stopped for cupcakes at *Pinkitzel (150 NE K Gaylord Blvd.)*, before passing by more than 300 banjos in the *American Banjo Museum*.

In the very center of town, a crowd had gathered for the topping-off ceremony of the city's newest tallest building, the *Devon Tower*.

Opposite, the beautiful *Myriad Botanical Gardens* cover a huge area, with a giant cylindrical greenhouse as the centerpiece. You can learn about everything Cowboy and Western at the *National Cowboy & Western Heritage Museum*, with many of John Wayne's guns on display.

POST | CARD

Cyrus Avery, from Tulsa, lobbied Congress in the 1920s to pave Route 66 end to end from *Chicago* to *Los Angeles*. The highway was heavily promoted, and grew to be the most popular road for travelers heading west. Roadside attractions sprang up across the route—a giant blue sperm whale in *Catoosa*, a bronze sculpture where east meets west in *Tulsa*,

and *OK Country 66*, with replicas of many classic roadside landmarks. Oklahoma's stretch of it has one of our favorite stops—*Pops (660 W. Highway 66)*. Next to a 66ft (20m)-high soda bottle sculpture, the café has more than 600 varieties of pop, in every flavor imaginable. And a gas station, in case the car gets thirsty too!

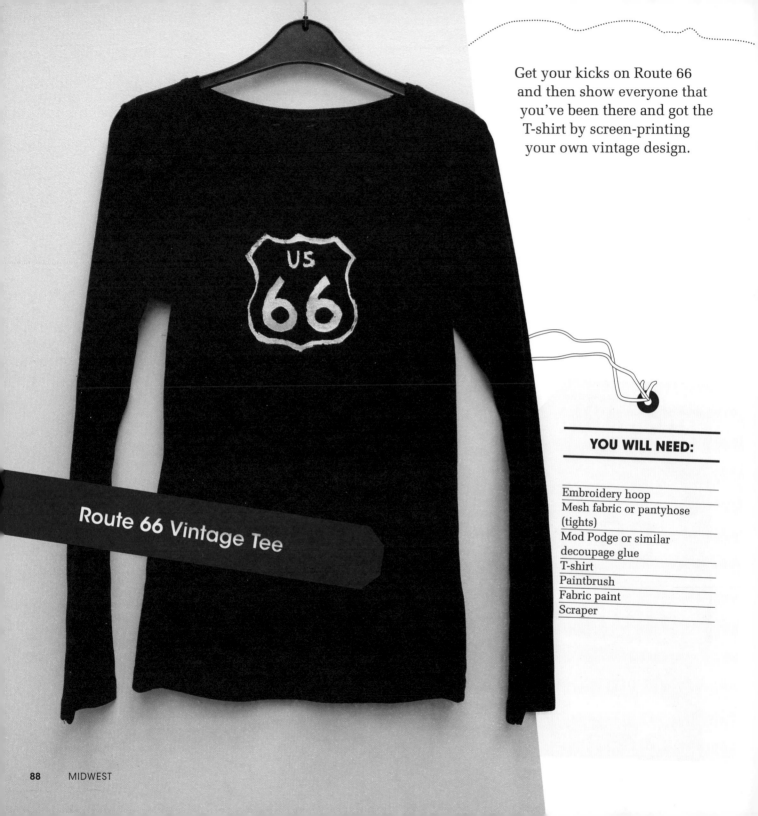

Get your kicks on Route 66 and then show everyone that you've been there and got the T-shirt by screen-printing your own vintage design.

Route 66 Vintage Tee

YOU WILL NEED:

Embroidery hoop
Mesh fabric or pantyhose (tights)
Mod Podge or similar decoupage glue
T-shirt
Paintbrush
Fabric paint
Scraper

STEP 1 Pick a design you'd like to put on your T-shirt and scale it to fit inside your embroidery hoop.

STEP 2 Tightly stretch the piece of mesh fabric inside your embroidery hoop and cut off any excess.

STEP 3 Trace the design on to the fabric with a pen.

STEP 4 Paint all the areas that aren't part of your design with Mod Podge. You can check if you've missed any patches by holding it up to the light.

STEP 5 Leave it to dry for several hours.

STEP 6 Lay the T-shirt on a flat surface and position the embroidery hoop on top.

STEP 7 Squeeze a small line of fabric paint down one side and use the scraper to spread the paint evenly across the design.

STEP 8 Carefully remove the frame and run it under the tap to remove the paint. Let the paint dry before trying on your new T-shirt!

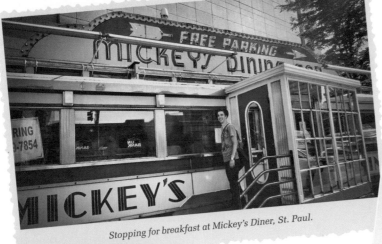

Stopping for breakfast at Mickey's Diner, St. Paul.

Gold Medal Flour sign on the riverside, Minneapolis.

Good service at The Bad Waitress, Minneapolis.

Mall of America.

Vegetarian sloppy joes at The Bad Waitress.

Minneapolis riverfront.

MiNNeSotA

Known as the Land of 10,000 Lakes, Minnesota actually has more than 11,000. Of course, this causes more than a few naming problems, with 150 "Long Lakes" and 200 "Mud Lakes"!

Our trip took us to the Twin Cities of *Minneapolis* and *St. Paul*, where we stopped for breakfast at *Mickey's (36 West 7th St.)*, an Art Deco diner that has been open 24 hours non-stop since 1939. We loved Claes Oldenburg's *Spoonbridge and Cherry*, just one of the artworks at the *Minneapolis Sculpture Garden*, and the lawn-mowing rock-men at the courthouse were adorable. The Mississippi runs right through the heart of the city and the views from the riverfront are amazing, with giant lettered signs on top of many of the buildings. We passed several groups of tourists sightseeing their way around the city. Local-born musician Prince still owns *First Avenue and 7th St.*, a concert venue and bar covered in painted stars for each of the artists who've played there.

Occupying almost 100 acres (40 hectares) near the airport, the 520 stores of the *Mall of America* attract twice as many visitors as the Twin Cities. Just spending 10 minutes in each store would take 86 hours—so we skipped a couple of stores to head back on the highway for some lunch at *The Bad Waitress Café (2 E. 26th St.)*. Our favorite store was *I Like You (501 1st Ave. NE)*, full of cute gifts and jewelry.

The next morning, we had delicious waffles at *Birchwood Café (3311 E. 25th St.)*; the smallest restaurant in the city—the 10ft (3m)-wide *Al's Breakfast (413 14th Ave. SE)*, with only 14 seats—was (understandably) full up!

Breakfast at the Birchwood Café, Minneapolis.

Roll-up Shopping Tote

This project is a license to print money … on your very own shopping tote. Fold it up to look like a wad of fresh bills. Or, unroll and fill up with your shopping. We're sure it'd work great at the Mall of America!

YOU WILL NEED:

Rubber for stamp
Cotton or muslin (calico)
Fabric paint
White elastic
Carving tools
Sewing machine

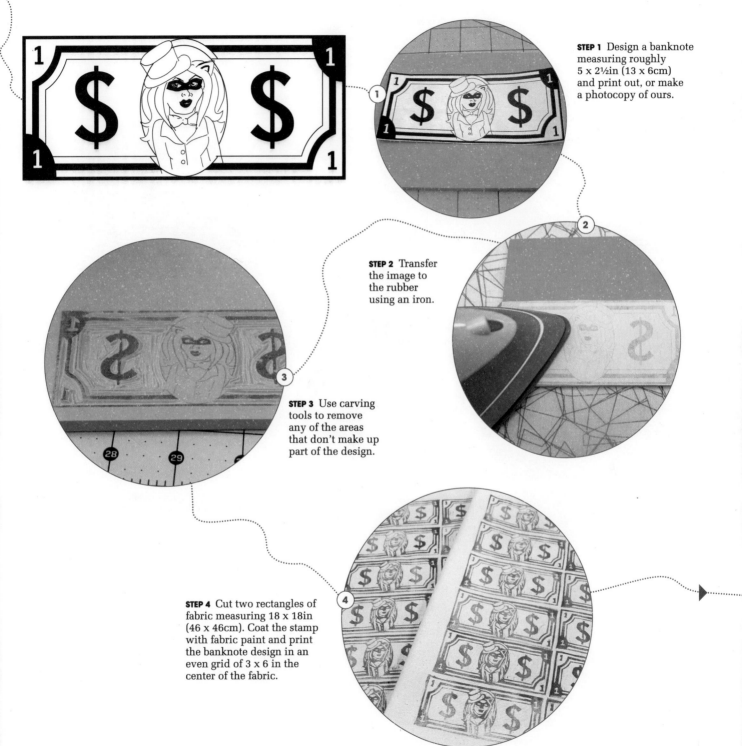

STEP 1 Design a banknote measuring roughly 5 x 2½in (13 x 6cm) and print out, or make a photocopy of ours.

STEP 2 Transfer the image to the rubber using an iron.

STEP 3 Use carving tools to remove any of the areas that don't make up part of the design.

STEP 4 Cut two rectangles of fabric measuring 18 x 18in (46 x 46cm). Coat the stamp with fabric paint and print the banknote design in an even grid of 3 x 6 in the center of the fabric.

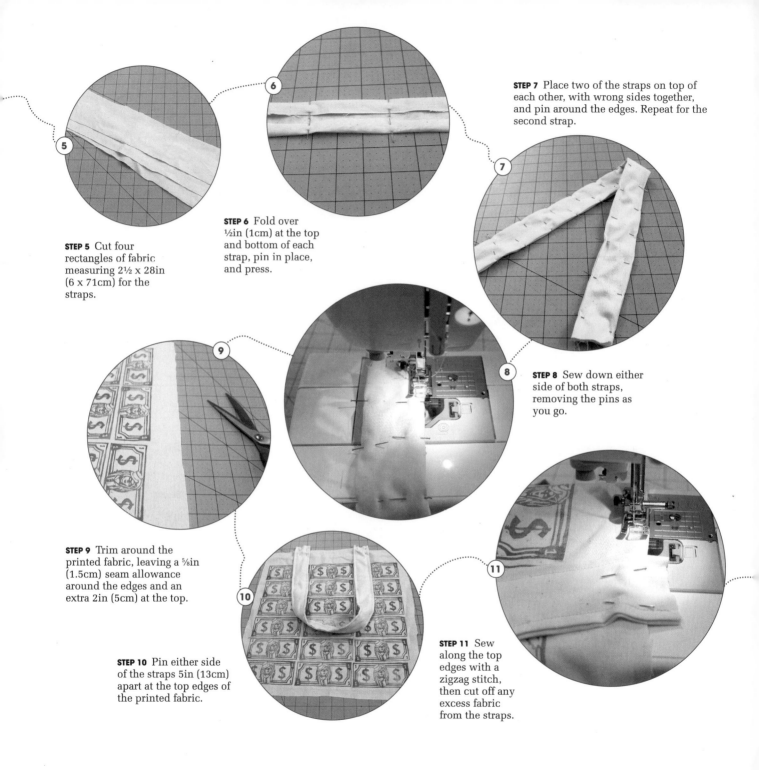

STEP 5 Cut four rectangles of fabric measuring 2½ x 28in (6 x 71cm) for the straps.

STEP 6 Fold over ½in (1cm) at the top and bottom of each strap, pin in place, and press.

STEP 7 Place two of the straps on top of each other, with wrong sides together, and pin around the edges. Repeat for the second strap.

STEP 8 Sew down either side of both straps, removing the pins as you go.

STEP 9 Trim around the printed fabric, leaving a ⅝in (1.5cm) seam allowance around the edges and an extra 2in (5cm) at the top.

STEP 10 Pin either side of the straps 5in (13cm) apart at the top edges of the printed fabric.

STEP 11 Sew along the top edges with a zigzag stitch, then cut off any excess fabric from the straps.

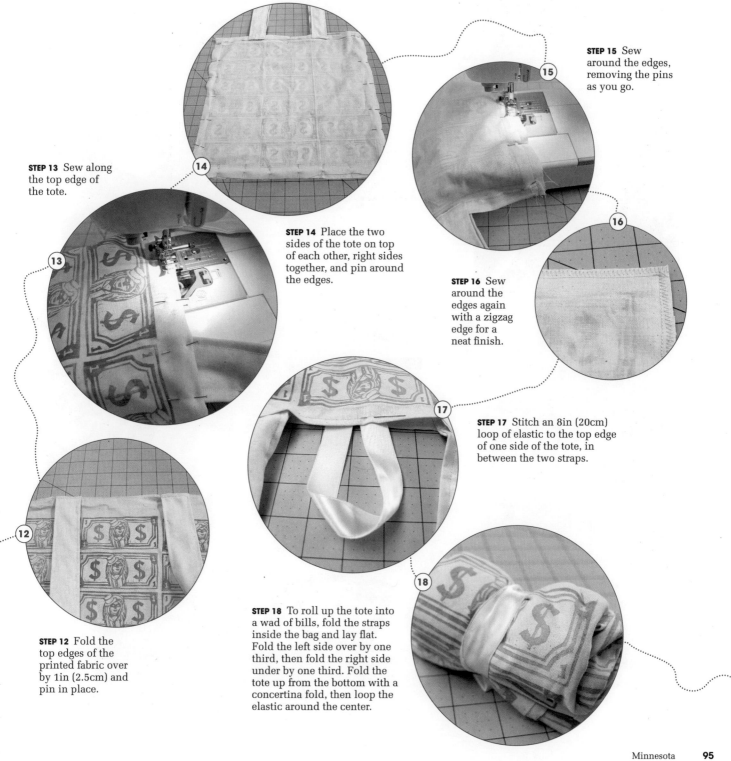

STEP 15 Sew around the edges, removing the pins as you go.

STEP 13 Sew along the top edge of the tote.

STEP 14 Place the two sides of the tote on top of each other, right sides together, and pin around the edges.

STEP 16 Sew around the edges again with a zigzag edge for a neat finish.

STEP 17 Stitch an 8in (20cm) loop of elastic to the top edge of one side of the tote, in between the two straps.

STEP 12 Fold the top edges of the printed fabric over by 1in (2.5cm) and pin in place.

STEP 18 To roll up the tote into a wad of bills, fold the straps inside the bag and lay flat. Fold the left side over by one third, then fold the right side under by one third. Fold the tote up from the bottom with a concertina fold, then loop the elastic around the center.

Pie shake at the Hamburg Inn, Iowa City.

Cat meets a squirrel in Council Bluffs, Iowa.

Filling up at the World's Largest Truckstop.

Tuck into a zombie burger, Des Moines.

A bank robbed by Bonnie & Clyde.

Giant glasses at the Buddy Holly Memorial in Clear Lake.

IOWA

The Midwest, and Iowa in particular, are sometimes referred to as the Flyover States—only encountered by most Americans as they travel from one side of the country to the other. But Iowa is *definitely* best seen from the ground. Our trip started in *Council Bluffs*, the black squirrel capital of the world.

Farther east, after passing a bank once robbed by Bonny and Clyde in *Stuart*, and a cemetery in the middle of a traffic circle, we arrived at our first stop, *Des Moines*. We had lunch at the *Zombie Burger + Drink Lab (300 E. Grand Ave.)*, a zombie-themed burger bar. Geeks will love *Cup O'Kryptonite (2608 Beaver Ave.)*, where you can grab the latest issue of your favorite comic while ordering a drive-through coffee. Or, if that's not your style, grab a cake or enjoy brunch at *La Mie Bakery (841 42nd St.)*.

Just north of the city lies *Clear Lake*, a picturesque little town where Buddy Holly played his last gig before his tragic plane crash with the Big Bopper. We visited a pair of giant glasses that mark the start of the trail to the crash site, after a coffee while sitting in a horse saddle at the *Cabin Coffee Company (303 Main Ave.)*.

POST | CARD

Back on the road, we passed the *World's Largest Truckstop* on our way to *Iowa City*, where we stopped at the *Hamburg Inn (214 N. Linn St.)* for a snack and drink in one, in the form of a pie shake. A whole slice of pie is blended together with ice cream, and one glass was too much for both of us to finish.

Every four years, Iowa becomes the focus of national attention as home to the Iowa caucus, as it becomes the first state for political parties to choose their presidential candidate. Ronald Reagan, Bill Clinton, and Barack Obama have all stopped by the Hamburg Inn while campaigning.

Propaganda at the Hamburg Inn, Iowa City.

Inspired by our visit to the Hamburg Inn, we're going to whip up a pie shake using a slice of pecan pie. Personalize yours by using your favorite flavor of pie matched with your favorite ice cream!

Pie Shakes

INGREDIENTS:

For the pie:

6oz (170g) pie crust (pastry shell), blind baked
3½oz (100g) pecans
2 eggs
6oz (170g) golden (light corn) syrup
3½oz (100g) superfine (caster) sugar
½ stick (55g) butter, melted
2 tbsp brown sugar
1 tsp vanilla
Pinch of salt

For the shake:

2 scoops of chocolate ice cream
3½ fl oz (100ml) milk
Whipped cream
Sprinkles
Cherries

STEP 1 Preheat the oven to 325°F (gas mark 3/170°C). Place the pie crust on a cookie sheet (baking tray) and fill with pecans.

STEP 2 Whisk together the remaining ingredients until smooth and creamy.

STEP 3 Pour the filling over the pecans in the pie crust and bake in the oven for 45 minutes until the filling is set and golden.

STEP 4 Leave the pie to cool for a little before cutting a generous slice for your shake.

STEP 5 Place the pie slice in a blender.

STEP 6 Add the ice cream and milk.

STEP 7 Blend until smooth.

STEP 8 Pour into a tall milkshake glass and top with whipped cream.

STEP 9 Top with sprinkles, cherries, and serve with two straws. You'll need a friend to help you drink it!

Iowa   99

"FM6 Walking Jackman" statue by Missourian Ernest Trova in Clayton, St. Louis.

Bud Alley on the Budweiser Brewery Tour, St. Louis.

The Blue Bird Bistro, Kansas City.

Tom admiring the view on the roof of the City Museum, St. Louis.

Soda bottling at Fitz's Soda, St. Louis.

Rocket on a building in Kansas City.

Missouri

Running from Kansas City to St. Louis before flowing into the Mississippi, the Missouri River runs right through the heart of the state that shares its name. With countless claims to fame (including the world's largest shuttlecock, pecan, and ball of videotape), it's no surprise that Missouri is also known as the Show Me State.

The land of present-day Missouri (and 15 other states) was part of the Louisiana Purchase acquired from the French in 1803. The subsequent exploration of the West by Lewis and Clark is celebrated by the *Gateway Arch* in their starting point, *St. Louis*. You can ride up the arch, or head over the river to Illinois for a spectacular view of the skyline.

A free tour of the *Budweiser* factory in downtown St. Louis will impress you with its sheer scale, as thousands of cans roll off the production line. If beer isn't your thing, grab an alcohol-free drink at *Fitz's (6605 Delmar Blvd.)*, where you can enjoy a tasty homemade soda as the 1940s mixing and bottling machines whirr away in the background.

The Gateway Arch and the St. Louis skyline.

City Museum is an old shoe factory that now houses a collection of explorable sculptures and art. Everything can be climbed—small passageways lead to hidden rooms, and a giant cavern holds a ten-story slide. On the roof, a Ferris wheel and more sculptures give you an amazing view over the city. It's one of the craziest places we've visited!

Tom outside the Budweiser packaging plant.

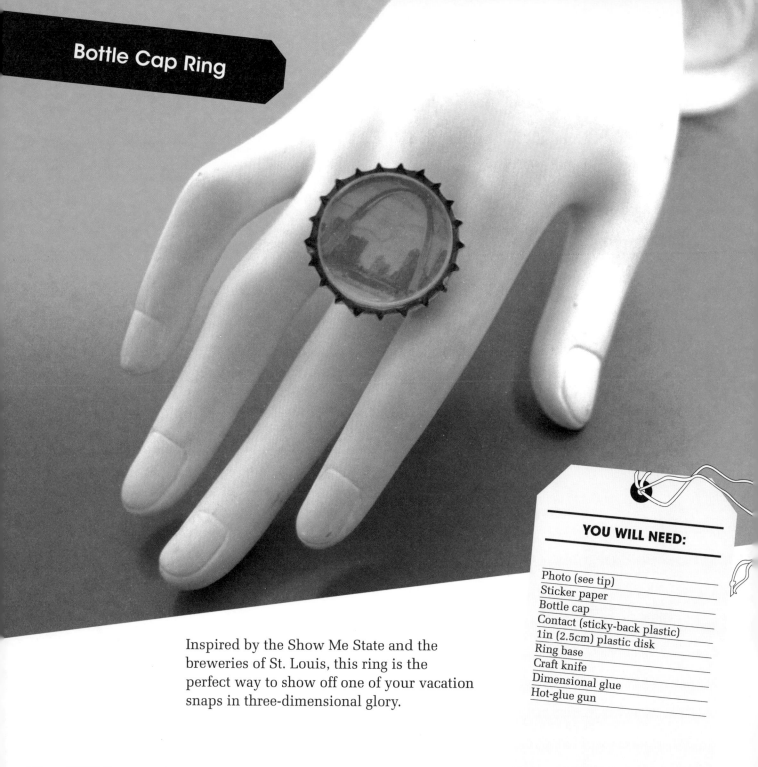

Bottle Cap Ring

Inspired by the Show Me State and the breweries of St. Louis, this ring is the perfect way to show off one of your vacation snaps in three-dimensional glory.

YOU WILL NEED:

Photo (see tip)
Sticker paper
Bottle cap
Contact (sticky-back plastic)
1in (2.5cm) plastic disk
Ring base
Craft knife
Dimensional glue
Hot-glue gun

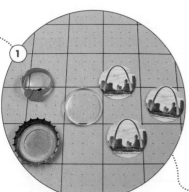

STEP 1 Print out the same photograph three or more times on to sticker paper, then cut these into 1in (2.5cm) circles.

TIP:

Choose a photo that has lots of depth, with a focal point in the middle. Clouds and city skylines work great.

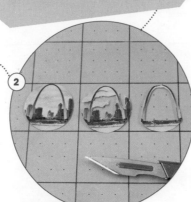

STEP 2 Using the craft knife, carefully cut out the background and middle ground from two of the photos.

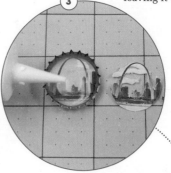

STEP 3 Stick the complete image into the bottle cap and cover with dimensional glue, leaving it to set.

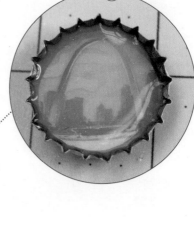

STEP 4 Stick your middle-ground photo into the ring, coat with another layer of glue, and leave to set.

STEP 5 Finally, stick your foreground photo into the ring and coat with one final layer of glue, leaving to set for several hours.

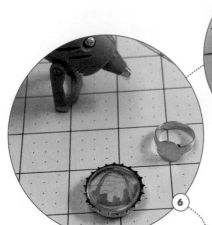

STEP 6 Cut out a 1in (2.5cm) circle of Contact and use it to secure the plastic disk inside the bottle cap.

STEP 7 Stick the ring base to the back of the bottle cap using the hot-glue gun and leave to cool.

Little Rock's little rock on the riverside.

Rocks & Stuff roadside rock shop.

Testing the water in Hot Springs. It's hot!

Friendly donkeys at the Alligator Farm and Petting Zoo.

Baby alligators, Alligator Farm and Petting Zoo.

Welcome to Hot Springs

Home town of Bill Clinton

Hot Springs is proud of its most famous native—President Bill Clinton.

Mountain Tower, at the top of Hot Springs Mountain.

ARKANSAS

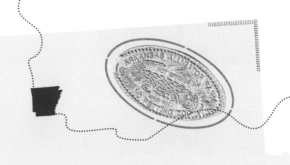

The perfect way to experience the Natural State is out in the sticks. And, if nature happens to call while you're in the *Dover* area, you can try out the *World's Only Double-Decker Outhouse (Booger Hollow Trading Post, 28858 Scenic Ark. 7).* Our first stop was the capital city of *Little Rock*, where we couldn't resist taking our photo with the town's namesake rock (which really was rather little) on the picturesque riverfront.

We continued along the interstate to *Hot Springs*, which was the boyhood home of Bill Clinton. Once a haven for gangsters and gambling, today the town is still popular with tourists visiting the springs and historic spa hotels; its 4,000-year-old water is heated more than a mile below the earth's surface before gushing out of the natural springs. Numerous wax museums and souvenir stores line the main street, but we couldn't resist a trip around the *Arkansas Alligator Farm and Petting Zoo (847 Whittington Ave.),* where you can watch alligators from a safe distance and pet some softer, less toothy animals. If you don't have time to venture out to the springs themselves, there are numerous fountains in town where you can test out the steamy temperatures for yourself. We took in the gorgeous views of the town from the *Mountain Tower (401 Hot Springs Mountain Dr.)* before hitting the road.

Crossing the state on a rural highway, we had to do a double take when we passed by a roadside shack called *Jay's Crystal Bonanza (1024 US 270 E., Mt. Ida).* It was exactly as we expected, selling rocks in every shape and size. If you're feeling lucky, the *Crater of Diamonds State Park* in *Murfreesboro* lets visitors root around in a 37-acre (96-hectare) volcanic crater. If you discover a gem, it's finders, keepers!

Gator Crossing sign, Alligator Farm and Petting Zoo.

Old Shack Bird Box

Inspired by the Natural State, we're getting close to nature and turning twee into hillbilly with an old shack bird box.

YOU WILL NEED:

Sandpaper
Bird box
Silver paint
Bronze paint
Popsicle (ice lolly) sticks
Chalkboard paint
Chalk or chalk pen
Glue
Weatherproof varnish
Paintbrushes

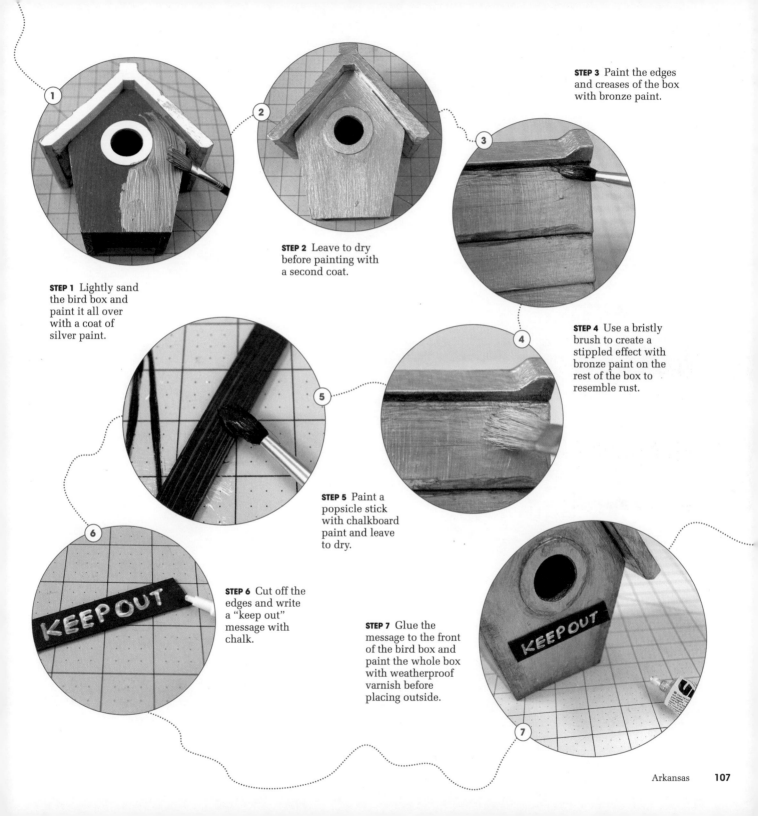

STEP 1 Lightly sand the bird box and paint it all over with a coat of silver paint.

STEP 2 Leave to dry before painting with a second coat.

STEP 3 Paint the edges and creases of the box with bronze paint.

STEP 4 Use a bristly brush to create a stippled effect with bronze paint on the rest of the box to resemble rust.

STEP 5 Paint a popsicle stick with chalkboard paint and leave to dry.

STEP 6 Cut off the edges and write a "keep out" message with chalk.

STEP 7 Glue the message to the front of the bird box and paint the whole box with weatherproof varnish before placing outside.

Extreme
Grilled
Cheeses

License Plate
Notebook

Tribune
Newspaper Nails

Food Truck
Napkin Holder

Drive-in
Movie Popcorn

WISCONSIN

MICHIGAN

ILLINOIS

INDIANA

OHIO

Bacon + Jam

Nacho

Mac'n'cheese

Popcorn

4

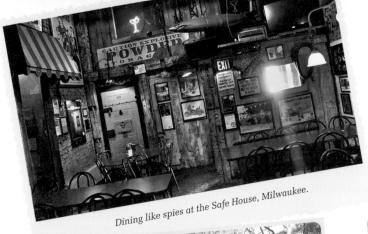

Dining like spies at the Safe House, Milwaukee.

A hobbit house!

Cows lining up in the car park at Kopp's Custard, Milwaukee.

Dancing feet at Ella's Deli.

Our night in a hot air balloon theme room at The Don Q Inn.

Stocking up on cheese at the Mousehouse, Madison.

The Bronze Fonz, Milwaukee.

WISCONSIN

Word travels fast about a good thing—and as we asked around about Wisconsin, we heard a lot about cheese! Known as America's Dairyland, Wisconsin produces more cheese per capita than any other state. We made sure to try some at the *Mars Cheese Castle (2800 W. Frontage Road, Kenosha)*, a crazy roadside stop selling everything dairy, and especially cheesy souvenirs.

We headed along the interstate to *Milwaukee*, home of *Harley-Davidson* and *Miller Beer*. Both offer tours, but we had a *top-secret* meal at *International Exports Ltd. (779 N. Front St.)*. Known as the *Safe House*, it's a spy-themed restaurant, full of hidden finds, espionage memorabilia, and a secret entrance. Our day got even happier with a visit to the *Bronze Fonz* sculpture next to the river. Eyyy!

Dairy made a second appearance in the form of frozen custard at a branch of *Kopp's (7631 W. Layton Ave., Greenfield)*. The addition of eggs makes it not quite ice cream, but similar, and it's become a delicious local specialty. Being fans of things that are really big or really small, we made one last stop on our way out of town to see an adorable little hobbit house in a housing estate called *The Shire*.

Over in *Madison*, the second largest city, we stopped for breakfast at *Ella's Deli and Ice Cream Parlor (2902 E. Washingtone Ave.)*, where *everything* moves—from the working train set in the table, to the hundreds of toys dangling from the ceiling. We made one last cheesy stop-off at the *Mousehouse Cheesehaus (4494 Lake Circle, Windsor)* to pick up some souvenirs before leaving the state.

"Insert cheesy joke here"!

Bacon+Jam Nacho Mac 'n' cheese

Extreme Grilled Cheeses

There's no wrong filling for a grilled cheese, just lots of options.

This American classic is easy to cook, and even more fun to adapt. We've tried a sweet-and-salty bacon and jelly flavor, a Southern-inspired smoky tortilla chip option, and classic mac 'n' cheese. Of course, try whatever you like—but you may find Wisconsin cheese works best!

Bacon, Avocado, and Jelly Grilled Cheese

Directions:

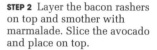

STEP 1 Butter two slices of bread. Lay slices of cheese on the unbuttered side of one of the slices.

STEP 2 Layer the bacon rashers on top and smother with marmalade. Slice the avocado and place on top.

STEP 3 Cook in a hot skillet (frying pan) until golden on the bottom.

STEP 4 Place the second slice of bread on top, butter side facing up, flip over, and cook until golden on the bottom.

STEP 5 Cut in half and serve hot.

INGREDIENTS:

Bread

3½oz (100g) English Wensleydale with apricots, or plain feta

3 bacon or meat-free rashers, broiled

Half an avocado

2 tbsp marmalade or jelly (jam)

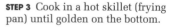

Smoked Tortilla Grilled Cheese

Directions:

STEP 1 Butter two slices of bread. Lay slices of cheese on the unbuttered side of one of the slices.

STEP 2 Sprinkle with tortilla chips and drizzle with a few drops of chipotle.

STEP 3 Cook in a hot skillet (frying pan) until golden on the bottom.

STEP 4 Place the second slice of bread, buttered side up, on top and flip over. Cook until golden on the bottom.

STEP 5 Cut in half and serve hot.

INGREDIENTS:

Bread

3½oz (100g) Applewood smoked cheddar, or any smoked hard cheese

Cheesy tortilla chips

Chipotle sauce

Mac 'n' Cheese Grilled Cheese

Directions:

STEP 1 Melt the butter in a saucepan and mix in the flour.

STEP 2 Whisk in the milk and leave to thicken for 15 minutes.

STEP 3 Meanwhile, cook the macaroni in a pan of boiling water.

STEP 4 When the sauce has thickened, shred (grate) half of the cheddar into the sauce and whisk until smooth.

STEP 5 Stir the cooked macaroni into the sauce.

STEP 6 Butter two slices of bread and top the unbuttered side of one slice with mac 'n' cheese.

STEP 7 Shred the remaining cheese on top.

STEP 8 Cook in a hot skillet (frying pan) until golden on the bottom.

STEP 9 Place the second slice of bread, buttered side up, on top and flip over. Cook until golden on the bottom.

STEP 10 Cut in half and serve hot.

INGREDIENTS:

½oz (10g) butter

½oz (10g) flour

7fl oz (200ml) milk

3oz (75g) macaroni

3½oz (100g) Wisconsin cheddar

Bread

Outside one of the stores in Wicker Park.

Crown Fountain water sculptures in Millennium Park, Chicago.

Get your secret agent supplies from The Boring Store, Chicago.

Rub Lincoln's nose for luck at his tomb in Springfield.

Meeting with a sock monkey in Rockford.

A giant Marilyn Monroe sculpture, Chicago.

ILLINOIS

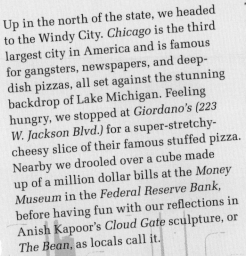

Our first stop in the Land of Lincoln was to rub the lucky nose of the man himself at the *Lincoln Tomb* in the capital, Springfield. The nose has turned a shiny bronze from all the eager tourists.

The view from the big wheel at Navy Pier, Chicago.

Up in the north of the state, we headed to the Windy City. *Chicago* is the third largest city in America and is famous for gangsters, newspapers, and deep-dish pizzas, all set against the stunning backdrop of Lake Michigan. Feeling hungry, we stopped at *Giordano's (223 W. Jackson Blvd.)* for a super-stretchy-cheesy slice of their famous stuffed pizza. Nearby we drooled over a cube made up of a million dollar bills at the *Money Museum* in the *Federal Reserve Bank*, before having fun with our reflections in Anish Kapoor's *Cloud Gate* sculpture, or *The Bean*, as locals call it.

The skyscrapers and huge mix of architectural styles make Chicago a striking city. An architecture cruise along the river is a fun way to explore it, but even from the ground, there's plenty to look at. Alternatively, give yourself vertigo as you stand suspended on a transparent balcony on the 103rd floor of the city's tallest building, *Willis Tower*. We took the more relaxing option of a ride on the carousel at *Navy Pier*, with an amazing view over the skyline and lake.

Creative types should jump on the "L" train to the *Wicker Park* area for a spot of shopping in *Quimby's Bookstore (1854 W. North Ave.)* and *Reckless Records (1532 N. Milwaukee Ave.)*, which was featured in the movie *High Fidelity*. The *Boring Store (1331 N. Milwaukee Ave.)* is anything but, selling everything a spy or secret agent could need, and if you're in the mood for some delicious vegan food, *The Chicago Diner (3411 N. Halsted St.)*

will fix you up. The city is filled with amazing art and sculptures, but *Oz Park* is an unusual find. Filled with statues from the famous book, it's a really pleasant place to stroll.

Our final stop in the state was *Rockford*, where we posed next to the town's most famous creation—sock monkeys!

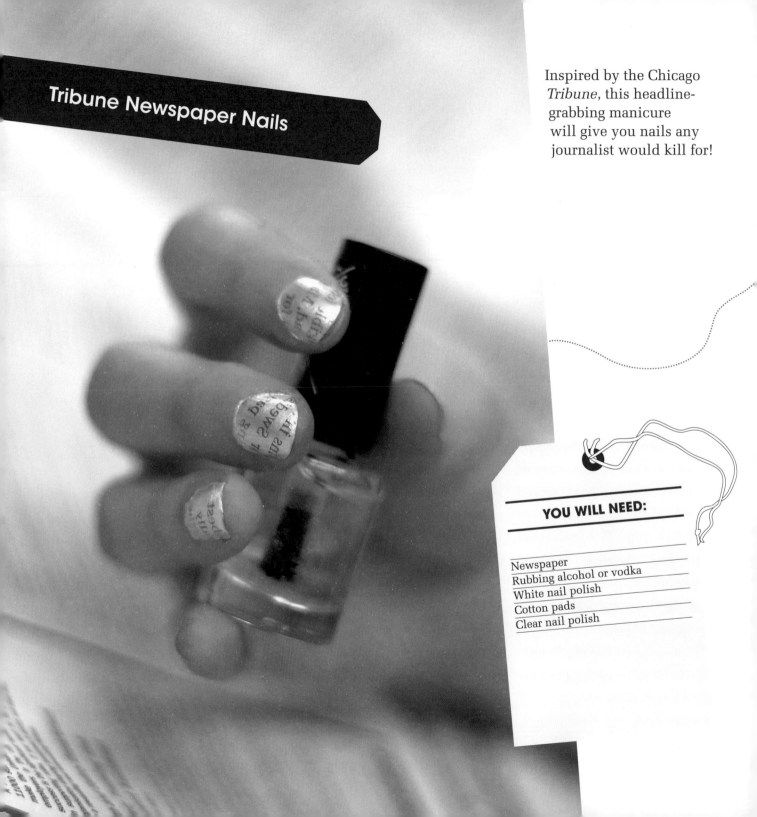

Tribune Newspaper Nails

Inspired by the Chicago *Tribune*, this headline-grabbing manicure will give you nails any journalist would kill for!

YOU WILL NEED:

Newspaper
Rubbing alcohol or vodka
White nail polish
Cotton pads
Clear nail polish

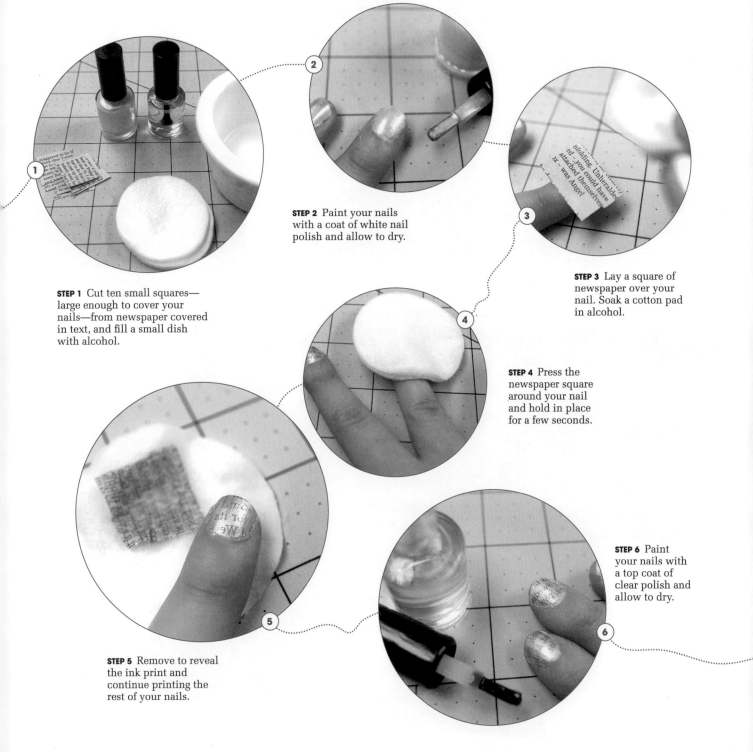

STEP 1 Cut ten small squares—large enough to cover your nails—from newspaper covered in text, and fill a small dish with alcohol.

STEP 2 Paint your nails with a coat of white nail polish and allow to dry.

STEP 3 Lay a square of newspaper over your nail. Soak a cotton pad in alcohol.

STEP 4 Press the newspaper square around your nail and hold in place for a few seconds.

STEP 5 Remove to reveal the ink print and continue printing the rest of your nails.

STEP 6 Paint your nails with a top coat of clear polish and allow to dry.

Twisty house at Artspark, Indianapolis.

The Children's Museum, Indianapolis.

Posing in a racing car at the Motor Speedway.

Hanging out at the Sunken Ship bar.

Outside Michael Jackson's childhood home in Gary.

The Borg-Warner trophy covered in winners of the Indianapolis 500.

There was a triple feature on at Tibb's Drive-In!

INDIANA

We began our Indiana adventure in *Gary*, and stopped by the childhood home of the King of Pop, Michael Jackson. Heading south through the Hoosier State (a nickname that has a handful of different explanations!), we reached the capital, *Indianapolis*.

Our first trip was to the *Motor Speedway*, where around 400,000 fans gather around the 2.5-mile (4km) track and watch cars reach speeds of more than 200 miles (320km) an hour. With a collection of winning cars spanning more than 100 years in the accompanying *Hall of Fame Museum*, there's a lot to take in. Even better, every winner of the Indy 500 gets a mini sculpture of their face added to the museum's Borg-Warner Trophy.

POST | CARD

We also enjoyed looking round the statues and sculptures at *Artspark* at the *Indianapolis Arts Center*, saw the amazing dinosaurs at the world's largest *Children's Museum*, and took a stroll along the canal in the center of town.

When we were planning our trip, place names like *Popcorn*, *Pidgeon*, *Licking*, and even *Santa Claus* sounded like perfect stop-off points, but we stuck

with something closer to home—*Edinburgh*—and filled up with snacks from *Not Just Popcorn (114 E. Main Cross St.)*. All that popcorn comes in handy: Indiana has more interstate per square mile than any other state, which led to the establishment of more than 120 drive-in theaters. Nowadays, 23 are still up and running.

Drive-in Movie Popcorn

After a long day on the road, there's nothing better than a good movie or three. Even better, if you find a classic drive-in theater, you don't even have to leave the car.

Our favorite thing was the triple feature. We've come up with a few popcorn toppings to match the mood of each genre. Just don't get the popcorn down the seats!

ROMANCE—THESE TREATS ARE AS GOOEY AS YOUR HEART.

¼ cup (50g) popping corn
½ cup (80g) flaked almonds
¼ cup (40g) Turkish delight, chopped
3½oz (100g) marshmallows
1 tsp rose essence
½ tsp lavender essence
Crushed rose petals
2oz (50g) bittersweet (dark) chocolate

Pop the popcorn and lay flat in a baking tray or similar. Sprinkle over the almonds and chopped Turkish delight. Melt the marshmallows in a double boiler and stir in the rose essence, lavender essence, and crushed rose petals. Drizzle over the popcorn. Finally, melt the chocolate and drizzle on top.

HORROR—GUARANTEED TO KEEP THE VAMPIRES AWAY. WE'RE JUST NOT SURE IT WORKS ON ZOMBIES...

¼ cup (50g) popping corn
6 tbsp butter
2 tbsp tomato puree (paste)
2 tbsp Worcester sauce
2 cloves of garlic, minced
4 tsp chili powder
2 tsp cayenne pepper
2 tsp onion granules
2 tsp chili flakes
¼ lime

Pop the popcorn and spread out in a baking tray. Melt the butter in a saucepan and stir in the tomato puree, Worcester sauce, and garlic. Drizzle over the popcorn and dust with the chili powder, cayenne pepper, onion granules, and chili flakes. Squeeze the lime juice over and serve.

ACTION—FOR AN EXPLOSIVE TIME.

¼ cup (50g) popping corn
4 Oreo cookies, crumbled
½ cup (100g) M&Ms
4 tbsp butter, melted
½ cup (115g) sugar
½ tsp sea salt
1 pack popping candy

Pop the popcorn and lay flat in a baking tray. Sprinkle over the crumbled cookies and M&Ms. Drizzle the butter over the popcorn. Melt the sugar in a saucepan until caramelized, add the salt, and drizzle over the popcorn. Sprinkle the popping candy on top and serve.

SS-100-X—the limousine in which JFK was assassinated.

The make-your-own hot dog exhibit, Henry Ford Museum.

Choosing our ice cream toppings in Hell.

Downtown Detroit.

Our warm welcome to Hell, MI.

The famous Fox Theatre in Detroit.

The seat from Ford's Theatre, where Abraham Lincoln was assassinated in 1865.

MiCHiGAN

Made up of two peninsulas between four Great Lakes, Michigan is undoubtedly most famous as the home of the automobile industry. Ford, GM, and Chrysler are all based in the *Detroit* area. Our first stop was the *Henry Ford Museum* in *Dearborn*, an incredible collection of exhibits collected by the pioneer of mass production. It features everything from the chair that Abraham Lincoln was assassinated in and the Wienermobile (a hot-dog-shaped car), to Rosa Parks's bus and a huge collection of presidential cars. Even Thomas Edison's last breath is preserved!

Downtown Detroit has suffered from a declining population and huge poverty since the city's boom time in the early twentieth century. However, crafters and photographers will be inspired by *The Heidelberg Project (3600 Heidelberg St.)*, where an entire street of foreclosed houses have been painted and decorated by local artists.

POST CARD

We can't resist a good pun, and when we heard that going to *Hell* and back was possible (and that we could stop off for ice cream), we had to make a detour. After a few scoops and a visit to the Coffin of Toppings at *Scream's Ice Cream (4045 Patterson Lake Rd.)* we hit the road again. There was even a meet-up of heavy-metal hearse owners during our visit!

Unsure if the devil had a role to play, our car got a flat tire and we had to make an unscheduled pit stop in the college town of *Ann Arbor*. Luckily we ended up stranded in the parking lot of *Zingerman's Roadhouse (2501 Jackson Ave.)*, where we got to tuck into mac 'n' cheese and order coffee from the drive-through teapot while waiting for a mechanic.

Toy-covered house in The Heidelberg Project, Detroit.

License Plate Notebook

Inspired by Motown, this project is great if you have an old license plate. You can also pick one up from an antiques store, or online. There are hundreds to choose from, so look out for older plates with interesting designs and slogans. We picked out a retro Michigan plate from the 1970s. Use it as a travel journal—it'll withstand the toughest of road trips!

YOU WILL NEED

License plate
Oven cleaner/polish
Duct tape
Magnets
Small notepad and pen
Dremel/small angle grinder, drill, or similar
Metal file
Craft knife

STEP 10 Slip the notepad in the pocket, slide the pen through the loop, and decorate the inside of your notebook with stickers and travel mementos.

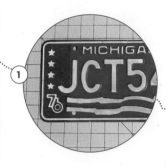

STEP 1 Begin by giving the license plate a clean to make it shine. We used soapy water to clean the front, and oven cleaner to remove all the dirt from the back.

STEP 2 Mark lines at 4¼in (11cm), 4¾in (12cm), 9in (23cm), and 9½in (24cm).

STEP 3 Carefully cut the license plate along these lines using your chosen power tool.

STEP 4 File down any sharp edges on each piece thoroughly.

STEP 5 Place the pieces alongside each other, and tape together with strips of duct tape.

STEP 6 Tape down magnets on the flap. If you have an aluminum plate and the magnets don't stick, you'll need to place a second set of magnets on the inside flap too.

STEP 8 Trim off any excess tape with the craft knife.

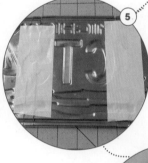

STEP 7 Cover the entire back with strips of duct tape.

STEP 9 Make a pocket for the notepad by taping together strips of duct tape to create two 4 x 5in (10 x 12.5cm) rectangles and stick them together. Fold a 4in (10cm) strip of tape in half lengthways and trim before placing along the top of the pocket to create a loop for a pen. Tape either side of the pocket to the back of the notepad.

Crafty goodies at Wholly Craft, Columbus.

Salad in a bread bowl at the Indigo Café, Cincinnati.

Pancakes at Big Boy, Columbus.

Tom got hungry!

The Coffee Emporium in Cincinnati was just what two worn-out roadtrippers needed!

We had a cocktail from the Surly Girl Saloon in Columbus.

OHio

After rolling into *Columbus* on three wheels and a spare tire, we discovered that you're never too far from a good diner where you can kill time. We relaxed with breakfast at one of the *Big Boy Restaurants* as the mechanics did their work. Back on the road, we headed to the trendy *Short North* area and grabbed a drink at the *Surly Girl Saloon (1126 N. High St.)*, which is decked out like a cowgirl's watering hole and sells a range of woman-brewed beers, before going craft shopping in *Wholly Craft (3169 N. High St.)*.

Emblazoned on Ohio's license plate is "Birthplace of Aviation Pioneers," aggravating its rivalry with North Carolina—though the Wright brothers were *born* in the state, they made their first flight at Kitty Hawk, NC. However, Ohioans have reached a lot higher than the 10ft (3m) of Orville and Wilbur: The first American to orbit the Earth (John Glenn), the first man on the Moon (Neil Armstrong), and 22 other astronauts all come from Ohio.

Back on land, we headed south to *Cincinnati*, where we passed the *Mushroom House (3331 Erie Ave.)*, an incredible one-bedroom house in the shape of a mushroom, designed by architect Terry Brown. It's near a *really* great latte at *The Coffee Emporium (110 E. Central Pkwy.)*. If you haven't spotted enough signs on your road trip, then a visit to the *American Sign Museum (1330 Monmouth Ave.)* is sure to fulfill your neon dreams.

The Mushroom House is a Cincinnati landmark built by architect Terry Brown.

Food Truck Napkin Holder

A food truck always has the perfect condiments, so why not park one up in your kitchen? These Airstream-style trailers were invented in Ohio, and many still crisscross the country as food trucks.

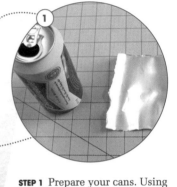

YOU WILL NEED:

Several aluminum cans. Larger ones work best

Black card

Contact (sticky-back plastic) (optional)

Cardboard

Duct tape

PVA glue

Rotary cutter and scissors

Awl

STEP 1 Prepare your cans. Using a knife or a can opener, remove the top and bottom. Then slice each can vertically, and unroll. Remove the shoulder of the can so you're left with a plain cylinder. Clean out any dregs!

STEP 2 Flatten it out by rubbing out the curve on a smooth surface. To make it extra flat, pop it between two cookie sheets (baking trays) in the oven for about 10 minutes at 300°F (gas mark 2/150°C).

STEP 3 Once you've got a few flat sheets, start to draw a template. To get the classic look, use smooth curves, or try rounded trapezoids for a more 1970s look. Make sure your design is wide enough to fit your napkins and condiments.

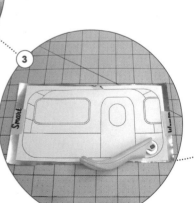

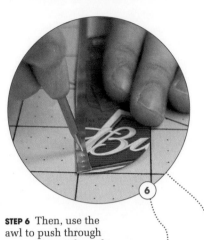

STEP 6 Then, use the awl to push through some "rivets" from the reverse side.

STEP 5 Add some structure by adding a panel along the bottom. Fold over the top of the piece to give it some depth.

STEP 7 Use the same technique for the window and doors. Add rivets along the edges, and fill in the window using black card. We added some Contact (sticky-back plastic) to give the windows a shine.

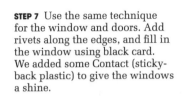

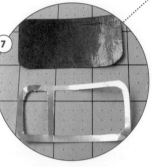

STEP 8 From the reverse of the main piece, draw some curves using the awl around the top to give a paneled effect.

STEP 9 Mark out the cardboard into a basic box pattern.

STEP 10 Cut out, and stick the sides together with duct tape. Don't worry about being too neat—it'll all be covered with the aluminum.

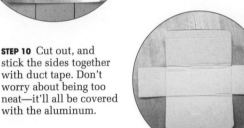

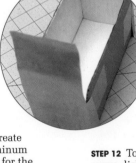

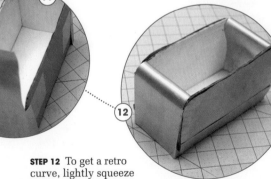

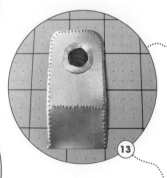

STEP 4 Build your truck by cutting out two matching base pieces. We found a cutting wheel works well to punch out the shapes.

STEP 11 Create two aluminum T-shapes for the front and back. Fold these around the box, and use PVA glue to stick them in place.

STEP 12 To get a retro curve, lightly squeeze the long flaps into the box and glue the front and back of the trailer in place.

STEP 13 Now, build up your design, affixing each piece with PVA glue. Fill with napkins, sauce, and whatever condiments you love!

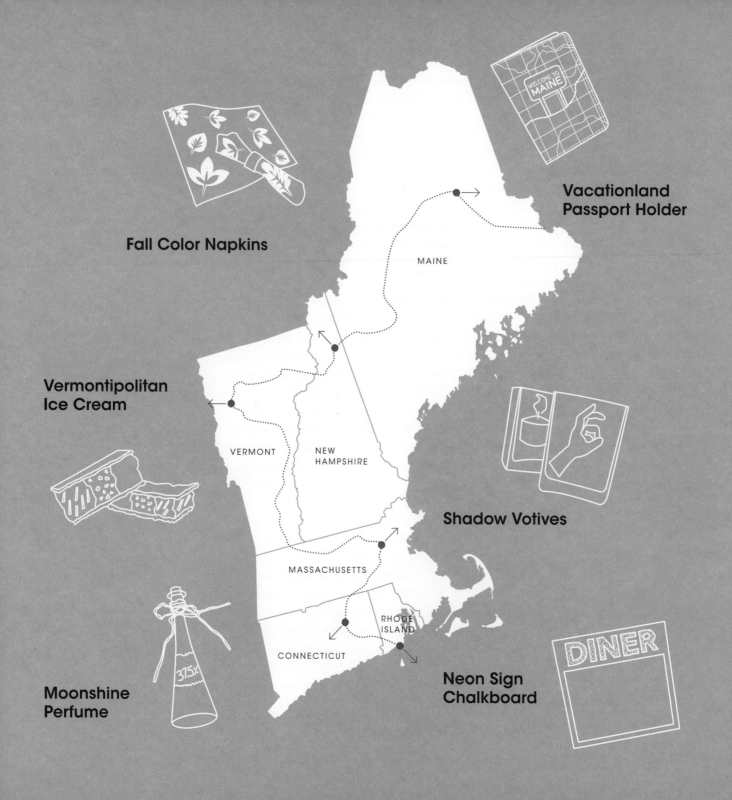

Fall Color Napkins

Vacationland Passport Holder

Vermontipolitan Ice Cream

Shadow Votives

Moonshine Perfume

Neon Sign Chalkboard

MAINE

VERMONT

NEW HAMPSHIRE

MASSACHUSETTS

RHODE ISLAND

CONNECTICUT

WELCOME TO MAINE

DINER

37.5%

Riding off into the sunset in Maine.

Exploring the streets of Portland.

A lunchbox full of menus and napkins at Silly's.

Breakfast at Silly's in Portland.

Tom tucking into his breakfast at Silly's.

Water tower in Maine.

Pretzel milkshake at Silly's.

MAINE

The most eastern state in the US, Maine is nicknamed Vacationland, and once you hear the locals, you'll be sure you're far from home. With words such as "anklebiter" for a young child, "ah-yah" for yes, and anyone not from the state coming from "away," you're sure to get a chuckle out of the lingo!

It's a big place—around 50 percent of the size of the whole New England area—but around a third of the population live near *Portland*. With 90 percent of the nation's lobster (locally known as "bugs") caught from the coast of Maine, you'll find all kinds of seafood in the restaurants here.

If crustaceans aren't your thing, *Silly's (40 Washington Ave.)* is a great stop for crazy decor and homemade food, while *Otto (576 Congress St.)* does a really delicious pizza. After a meal, you can clean up with a Maine-made toothpick—more than 90 percent of the US supply is made nearby.

Driving through the mountains in Maine.

The historic cobbled *Old Port* district is full of the town's maritime history and fishing piers. Off the coast, the *Acadia National Park* houses just one of the 60 lighthouses for which the state is famous.

A trip to *West Quoddy Head Light* in Lubec takes you to the very easternmost point of the US. Another six lighthouses are on the *Calendar Islands*, so-called because it was believed there were 365 of them—there are actually only a few over 200!

With only one syllable, and bordering only one other state, there's a lot that makes Maine unique.

Vacationland Passport Holder

YOU WILL NEED:

Card
Clear vinyl
Map (you can get these free at any Welcome Center)
Vacation photos
Glue
Sewing machine

Inspired by Maine's nickname, this holder will remind you of your adventures while keeping your passport in pristine condition.

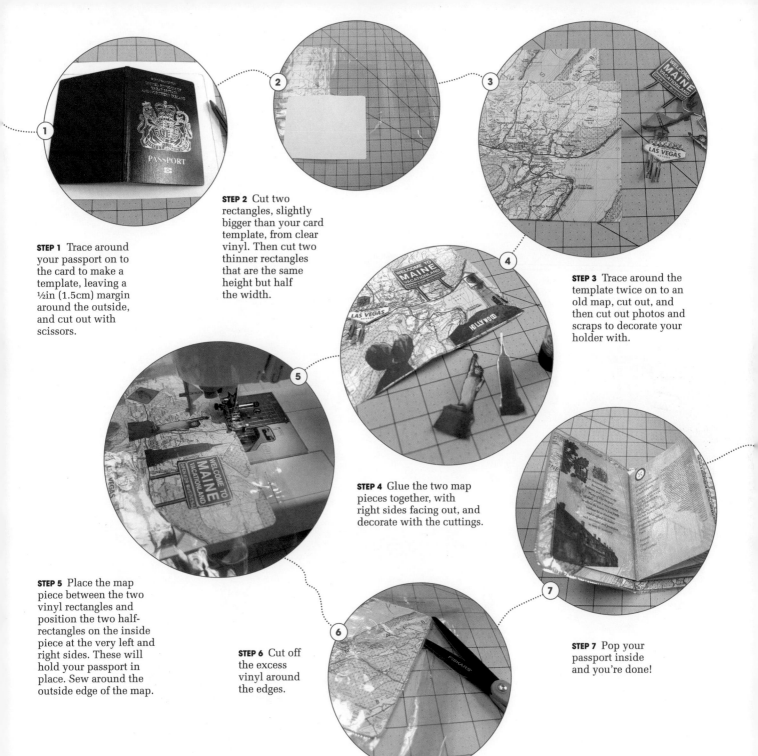

STEP 1 Trace around your passport on to the card to make a template, leaving a ½in (1.5cm) margin around the outside, and cut out with scissors.

STEP 2 Cut two rectangles, slightly bigger than your card template, from clear vinyl. Then cut two thinner rectangles that are the same height but half the width.

STEP 3 Trace around the template twice on to an old map, cut out, and then cut out photos and scraps to decorate your holder with.

STEP 4 Glue the two map pieces together, with right sides facing out, and decorate with the cuttings.

STEP 5 Place the map piece between the two vinyl rectangles and position the two half-rectangles on the inside piece at the very left and right sides. These will hold your passport in place. Sew around the outside edge of the map.

STEP 6 Cut off the excess vinyl around the edges.

STEP 7 Pop your passport inside and you're done!

Autumn leaves in New Hampshire.

A statue of war general John Stark, the "Hero of Bennington," in Manchester.

Thanksgiving pumpkins.

Exploring the streets of Portsmouth.

Watch out! There's a shark about in Portsmouth!

Driving north to see the fall leaf colors.

New Hampshire

"Live Free or Die" is one of the most memorable state mottos, and as the first state to break away from British rule, New Hampshire has an assertive and independent attitude.

POST CARD

On Columbus Day weekend in the fall, the state welcomes thousands of visitors from New York, Boston, and farther afield to view the amazing colors as the leaves change from green to golden brown. There's even an app to track the foliage across the state.

And for a bird's-eye view of the phenomenon, you can take a trip to the top of the state's highest peak, *Mount Washington*, on a cog railway, where winds have reached 200 miles (320km) per hour.

We stopped to sample fresh seafood in the coastal town of *Portsmouth*, with its cobbled streets and charming shops, before taking a scenic trip through the state to *Manchester*. Along the way the mountains, rivers, and sparkling waterfalls meant there was always something to look at. With theme parks such as *Story Land* and *Santa's Village*, numerous ski resorts, and the great heights of *Mount Washington* to scale, no wonder the state is so popular!

Welcome   Bienvenue

New Hampshire

"Live Free or Die"

Fall Color Napkins

YOU WILL NEED:

Muslin (calico)
Card
Green paint
Gold paint
Red paint
Clear shrink plastic
Cardboard tube (from foil or paper towel)
Contact (sticky-back plastic)
4 skeleton leaves
Sewing machine
Craft knife
Paintbrush

Perfect for your Thanksgiving table, these napkins will bring the fall colors to your dining table.

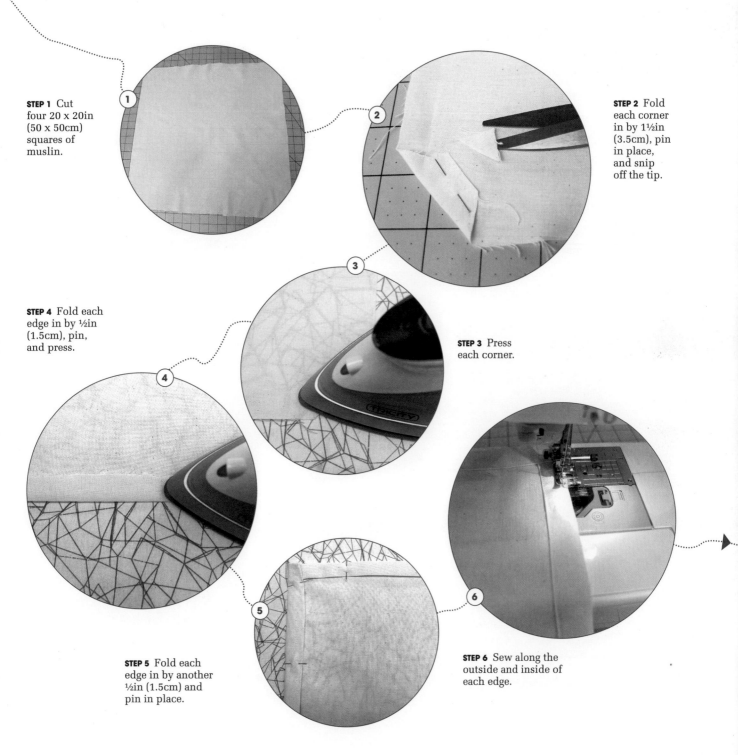

STEP 1 Cut four 20 x 20in (50 x 50cm) squares of muslin.

STEP 2 Fold each corner in by 1½in (3.5cm), pin in place, and snip off the tip.

STEP 4 Fold each edge in by ½in (1.5cm), pin, and press.

STEP 3 Press each corner.

STEP 5 Fold each edge in by another ½in (1.5cm) and pin in place.

STEP 6 Sew along the outside and inside of each edge.

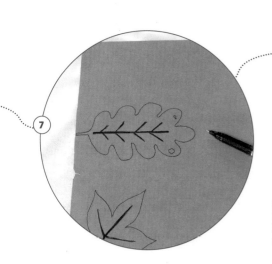

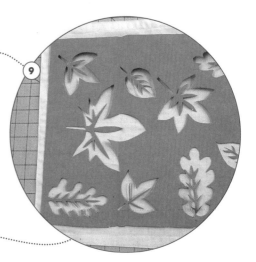

STEP 8 Carefully cut out the leaves with the craft knife, leaving the inner stalk attached.

STEP 7 Cut a sheet of card to the same size as your napkins and sketch some leaf designs.

STEP 9 Pin the stencil on top of a napkin.

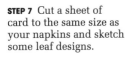

STEP 10 Paint the bottom of the leaves with green paint.

STEP 11 Paint the center of the leaves with gold paint, using the paintbrush edge to create a stippled effect.

STEP 12 Paint the top of the leaves with red paint, again creating a stippled effect.

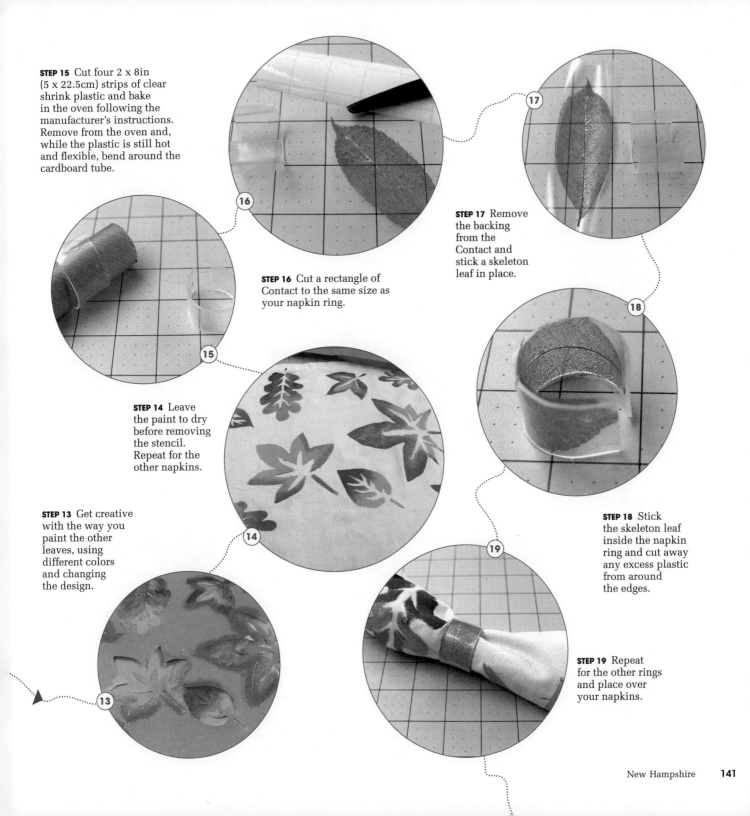

STEP 15 Cut four 2 x 8in (5 x 22.5cm) strips of clear shrink plastic and bake in the oven following the manufacturer's instructions. Remove from the oven and, while the plastic is still hot and flexible, bend around the cardboard tube.

STEP 17 Remove the backing from the Contact and stick a skeleton leaf in place.

STEP 16 Cut a rectangle of Contact to the same size as your napkin ring.

STEP 14 Leave the paint to dry before removing the stencil. Repeat for the other napkins.

STEP 13 Get creative with the way you paint the other leaves, using different colors and changing the design.

STEP 18 Stick the skeleton leaf inside the napkin ring and cut away any excess plastic from around the edges.

STEP 19 Repeat for the other rings and place over your napkins.

Learning about the history of Ben & Jerry's.

Our first plate of poutine!

Downtown Burlington.

An adorable baby moose.

Posing in an ice cream lid at Ben & Jerry's.

The World's Tallest Filing Cabinet.

Vermont

Alongside maple syrup, the Green Mountain State's most famous export is undoubtedly *Ben & Jerry's* ice cream. We stopped by the factory to try some samples, and took a tour of the "flavor graveyard," listing all their ex-flavors. We arrived late and ended up pacing around the graveyard in pitch darkness—luckily we're not scared of ice-cream-flavored ghosts! In the nearby town of *Burlington*, you can see where they opened their first store, with a plaque to commemorate it.

Although we didn't spot the *Lake Champlain Monster*, the legend hasn't put tourists off visiting the scenic area for skiing, snowsports, and ice fishing in the winter. Vermont borders Canada to the north, so keep an eye out for moose as you drive through the mountains. If you want to get a taste of Canada on this side of the border, there are plenty of places to try poutine (fries with cheese curds and gravy), including *Leunig's Bistro (115 Church St.)* or the

Bluebird Tavern (86 St. Paul St.) in *Burlington*. However, if you've got more of a sweet tooth, maple syrup is the perfect souvenir to take home. Vermont makes more maple syrup than any other state, and the *New England Maple Museum* in *Pittsford* is the perfect place to find out about the sticky substance.

One of the stranger roadside attractions we stopped at was the *World's Tallest Filing Cabinet*. A satirical sculpture built on the site of a proposed road, each drawer represents a year of the paperwork that the road project has created— it's *so* tall because the road was proposed back in 1965!

Ever wondered where old ice cream flavors go?

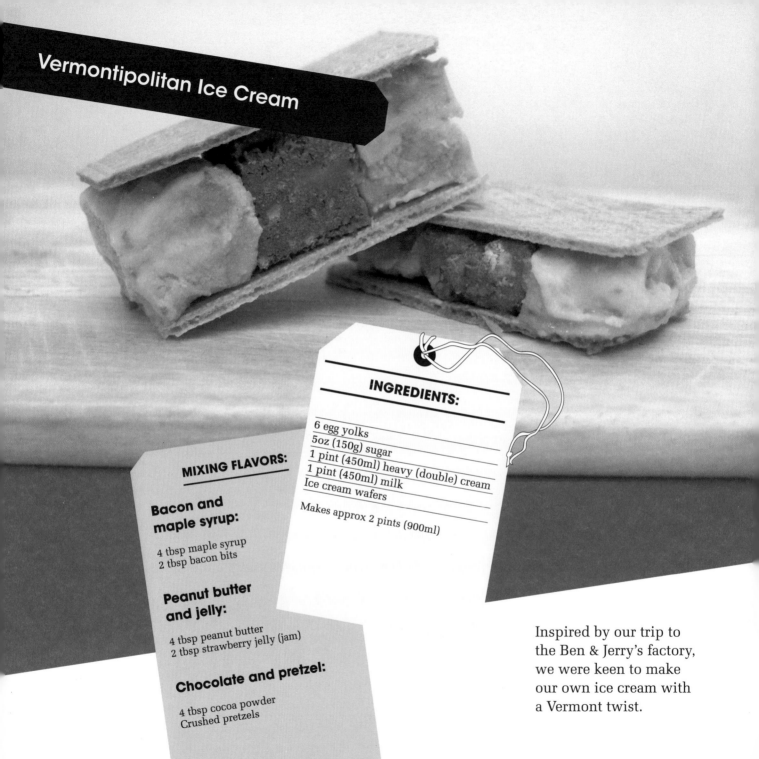

Vermontipolitan Ice Cream

INGREDIENTS:

6 egg yolks
5oz (150g) sugar
1 pint (450ml) heavy (double) cream
1 pint (450ml) milk
Ice cream wafers

Makes approx 2 pints (900ml)

MIXING FLAVORS:

Bacon and maple syrup:

4 tbsp maple syrup
2 tbsp bacon bits

Peanut butter and jelly:

4 tbsp peanut butter
2 tbsp strawberry jelly (jam)

Chocolate and pretzel:

4 tbsp cocoa powder
Crushed pretzels

Inspired by our trip to the Ben & Jerry's factory, we were keen to make our own ice cream with a Vermont twist.

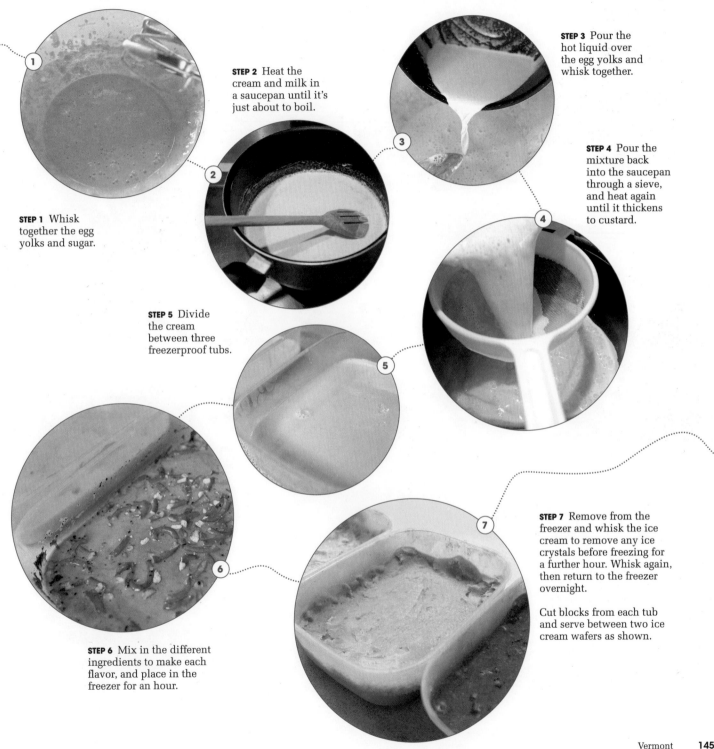

STEP 1 Whisk together the egg yolks and sugar.

STEP 2 Heat the cream and milk in a saucepan until it's just about to boil.

STEP 3 Pour the hot liquid over the egg yolks and whisk together.

STEP 4 Pour the mixture back into the saucepan through a sieve, and heat again until it thickens to custard.

STEP 5 Divide the cream between three freezerproof tubs.

STEP 6 Mix in the different ingredients to make each flavor, and place in the freezer for an hour.

STEP 7 Remove from the freezer and whisk the ice cream to remove any ice crystals before freezing for a further hour. Whisk again, then return to the freezer overnight.

Cut blocks from each tub and serve between two ice cream wafers as shown.

A breakfast cereal bar at Coven, Salem.

Spotting witches on water towers in Gallows Hill Park, Salem.

The port in Salem was once the sixth largest in the US.

Cat hanging out with the local witches in Salem.

The Boston skyline as we drove along I-95.

Tom takes a coffee break at Jaho Coffee & Tea, Salem.

Statue of Elizabeth Montgomery as Samantha Stephens from Bewitched, Salem.

MASSACHUSETTS

Along the Atlantic coast, the Bay State gave the world basketball and volleyball, but left it to Clarence Birdseye to provide a frozen meal before serving up the official dessert of Boston cream pie.

POST | CARD

Around *Boston* we had a great time, exploring the built-up downtown, before heading out to *Harvard Square*, home of the famous university, and birthplace of Facebook. We had some social-network-themed cupcakes at *Sweet (225 Newbury St.)* and took a look around the area,

followed by vegan pizza at *Peace o' Pie* (sadly closed for now). To get a great introduction to the city, the *Freedom Trail* passes 15 historic sites of the American Revolution before finishing across the Charles River at *Bunker Hill Monument*, a 221ft (67m)-high obelisk.

Have a Facebook cupcake next to Harvard University.

On a road trip, Boston doesn't do any favors for drive-by photographers—all major roads now run under the city after the US's most expensive highway project, *The Big Dig*, rerouted them in 2007.

We were excited to visit *Salem*, famous for the witch trials. The town is full of New Age and Wiccan boutiques. We followed the walking tour around the city, past the old port, and then on to *Gallows Hill*, where Bridget Bishop was hanged in 1692. Around town, you can pose with the *Bewitched* statue!

Shadow Votives

YOU WILL NEED:

Paper
Votive candleholders
Chalkboard paint
White paint
Candles
Black sand
Craft knife
Repositionable spray mount
Foam brush
Fine paintbrush

Inspired by the witchcraft of Salem, these candles cast a spooky shadow puppet on the wall. To avoid death by hanging, use only after 1693!

STEP 1 Take a photo of your hand making creepy shadow puppets on the wall and trace or sketch the design on paper.

STEP 2 Use the craft knife to cut out the design. Take care, as we'll be using the outline for the next step.

STEP 3 Use the spray mount to stick the templates to the front of the candleholders.

STEP 4 Using the foam brush, paint the shadows with chalkboard paint and leave to dry.

STEP 5 Paint with a second coat of chalkboard paint before removing the template, then use the knife to cut the paint from the gaps between the fingers.

STEP 6 With the fine paintbrush, paint the outline of the fingers with white paint.

STEP 7 Place the candles inside the holders and surround with black sand.

Heading into the state.

Retro PEZ advert at the PEZ museum.

PEZ everywhere—even under the floor!

Holy Land, an abandoned theme park inspired by stories from the Bible, Waterbury.

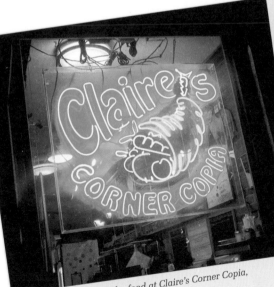
We loved the food at Claire's Corner Copia, New Haven.

Veggie burger at Claire's Corner Copia.

Connecticut

Less than 30 miles (48km) from Manhattan, the first of the New England states, Connecticut, is known as the Nutmeg State. We made our way along the interstate to *New Haven*, where *Yale University* started taking students more than 300 years ago. It's where Bill and Hillary Clinton met, and the town is full of students studying, hoping to find love, or become president! The vegetarian food at *Claire's Corner Copia (1000 Chapel St.)* was so good we stopped there twice.

Driving through Connecticut.

Another nickname is the Constitution State, as some believe that Connecticut's Fundamental Orders were the first written constitution in the world, and may even have provided the basis of the US Constitution. "Nutmeggers" have a history of invention. The method used to make car tires, the first dictionary, and the tape measure all originated here; the can opener was patented in *Waterbury* in 1858, more than 40 years after the invention of the can!

We visited the *PEZ Visitor Center* in *Orange*, where the small sweets and dispensers are made, though they weren't invented here.

If a PEZ doesn't hit the spot, the Onyx Spirits micro-distillery in *East Hartford* produces moonshine—in fact, Connecticut was one of two states not to ratify Prohibition, leading to speakeasies all over town.

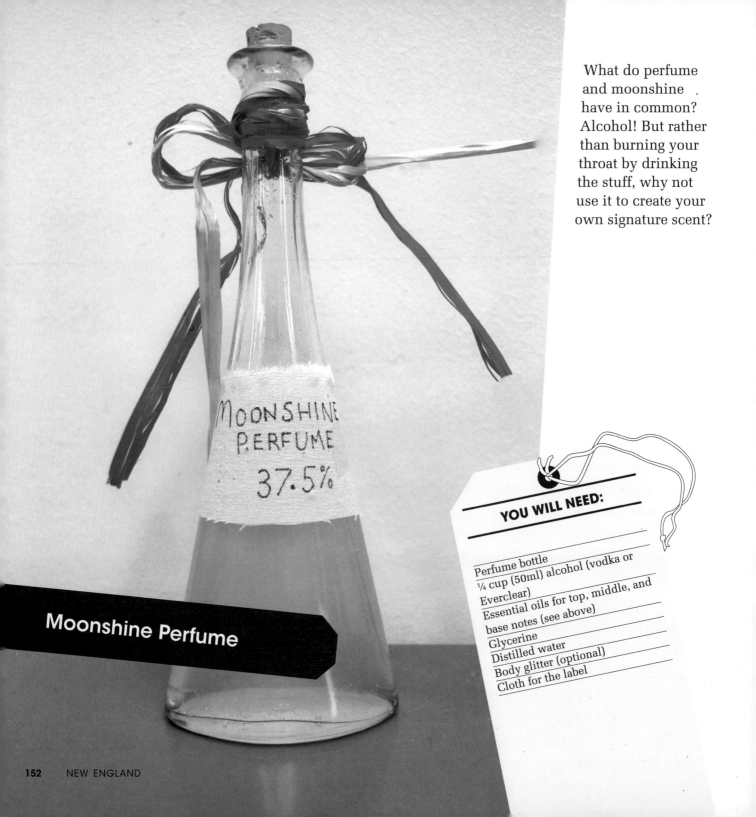

What do perfume and moonshine have in common? Alcohol! But rather than burning your throat by drinking the stuff, why not use it to create your own signature scent?

MOONSHINE PERFUME 37.5%

Moonshine Perfume

YOU WILL NEED:

Perfume bottle
¼ cup (50ml) alcohol (vodka or Everclear)
Essential oils for top, middle, and base notes (see above)
Glycerine
Distilled water
Body glitter (optional)
Cloth for the label

Choosing your scents:

Every perfume is made up from three different layers of scent: the **top note** (the first thing you smell when you spray a perfume), the **middle note** (which appears shortly after), and the **base note** (the base scent that remains on your skin). You'll make each note by mixing together different essential oils, and you'll want to experiment to come up with your own scent, but here are a few suggestions to get you started:

Base notes—cedarwood, rose, ginger, vanilla, frankincense, valerian, and sandalwood.

Middle notes—nutmeg, juniper, lavender, pine, rosemary, chamomile, clove, and ylang-ylang.

Top notes—cinnamon, mint, orange, lemon, lime, lemongrass, thyme, basil, and eucalyptus.

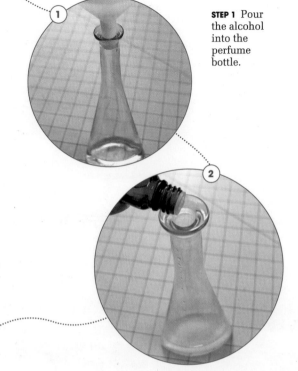

STEP 1 Pour the alcohol into the perfume bottle.

STEP 2 Add the scents, starting with the base notes, then the middle notes, and finally the top notes. Add 20–30 drops of each scent, shaking the bottle and smelling as you go to adjust the amounts to your liking. Keep a note of the quantities.

When you're happy with the scent, place the bottle in a cool, dark place for around one week to allow the perfume to age and the scents to become stronger.

STEP 3 After one week, test the perfume. If you like the smell, add a couple of drops of glycerine to preserve the scent. If you want to make some changes, add a few more drops of essential oil and leave to age for several more days before testing again.

STEP 4 Top up the perfume with distilled water. The amount you add will determine the strength of the perfume, so add less for a traditional perfume, or more for a body spray. You can also add a small amount of body glitter to give your perfume an added sparkle on the skin.

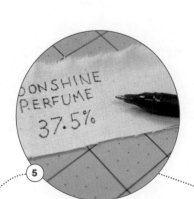

STEP 5 The final step is to name your perfume. For a rustic bootleg look, cut a rectangle of cloth for the label and write the name and alcohol percentage before gluing to the bottle.

Driving through Providence.

Monopoly signs in the parking lot of Hasbro HQ.

The Modern Diner, Providence.

Smartie pancakes for breakfast at the Modern Diner...

Tom meeting Mr. Potato Head outside Hasbro.

...we just managed to finish all of them!

RHODE ISLAND

At only 37 miles (60km) across and 48 miles (77km) long, there's no state smaller than Rhode Island—the Ocean State. *Narragansett Bay* connects the Atlantic to the state capital, *Providence*, creating more than 100 beaches on the way. Though the state was the first to break away from British rule, it was the last of the original states to sign the US Constitution.

POST | CARD

Our first stop was the *Modern Diner (364 E. Ave.)* in *Pawtucket*. Nowadays, it's anything but modern, but when it was built in the 1940s the streamlined design would have turned heads! The diner was a Rhode Island invention, when pies and coffee were sold to late-night workers by Walter Scott in 1872. Established in 1673 and still operating now, the oldest tavern—*The White Horse (26 Marlborough St.)* in *Newport*—is just one of hundreds of historic buildings in the state.

If you've got time, swing by the nearby *Hasbro* headquarters, park in a Monopoly square in the parking lot, and have your photo taken with Mr. Potato Head. Though small, Rhode Island fits a lot in!

Neon Sign Chalkboard

Bring a touch of diner kitsch to your kitchen with a piece of glow-in-the-dark string wall art in the style of a classic neon sign. The trickiest part is deciding what it's going to say!

YOU WILL NEED:

Square of MDF
White paint
Chalkboard paint
Nails
Red thread
Red embroidery floss
Masking tape
Paintbrush
Hammer

STEP 1 Start by marking on the MDF a square for the chalkboard, using masking tape.

STEP 2 Paint the surrounding area with white paint and let dry.

STEP 3 Paint the center square with chalkboard paint. You could use masking tape again for a clean edge.

STEP 4 Tape down a paper design or sketch the outline for the lettering along the top of the board, to help you work out your spacing.

STEP 5 Hammer nails along the outline and inside of each of the letters. Keep the spacing as even as possible, and try and align the nails in a neat pattern of squares.

STEP 6 Once you've hammered nails around the entire design, rip off the paper design or erase the outline.

STEP 7 Twist red thread around each of the nails, creating a grid design across the center of each of the letters.

STEP 8 Outline the letters by twisting red embroidery floss around the outside and inside edge of each.

STEP 9 Mount on the wall and enjoy!

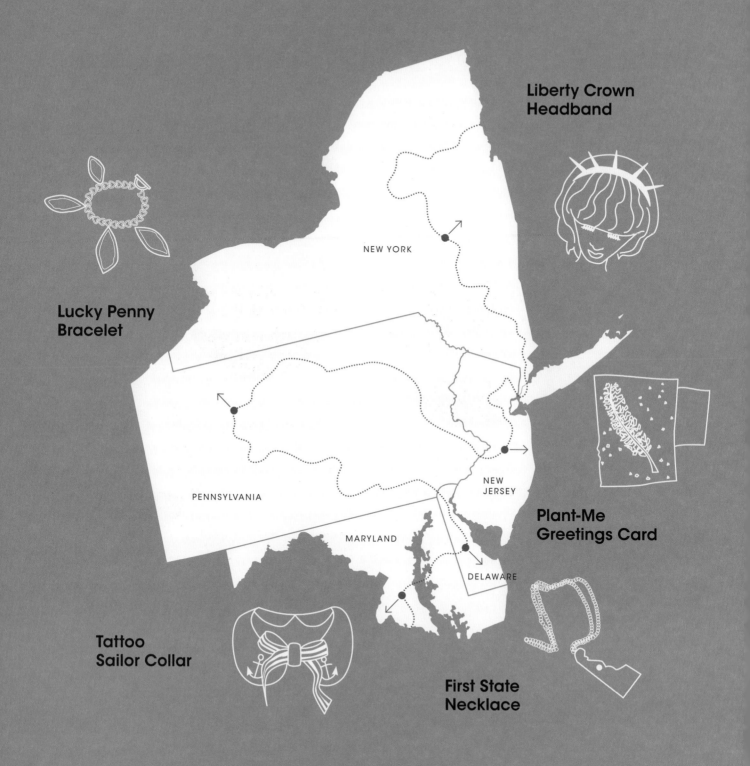

Liberty Crown
Headband

Lucky Penny
Bracelet

Plant-Me
Greetings Card

NEW YORK

PENNSYLVANIA

NEW
JERSEY

MARYLAND

DELAWARE

Tattoo
Sailor Collar

First State
Necklace

Top of the Rock, at 30 Rockefeller Plaza.

Taking a stroll along the High Line.

A UFO diner, Niagara Falls.

Rainbows at Niagara Falls.

Our favorite view of Manhattan from Dumbo.

Fifth Avenue and the Empire State Building.

The Statue of Liberty.

New York

Stretching from Niagara Falls down to the Big Apple, New York State is buzzing, busy, and full of the most famous landmarks in the world. It's easy to joke about Manhattanites never needing to leave the island, but it's easy to see why. The views from *Rockefeller Center* and the *Empire State Building* are breathtaking. We timed our visit for sunset and watched the city transform.

We loved *Dylan's Candy Bar (1011 3rd Ave.)* and *Magnolia Bakery (401 Bleecker St.)*. Over in Brooklyn, there really isn't a more impressive view than from *Dumbo*. Farther out, *Coney Island* is an old-time fairground on the seafront. On our visit, the beach was thick with snow! Of course, a "road trip" through the city quickly turns into six lanes of tailbacks and car horns—it's not for the faint-hearted.

A free trip on the *Staten Island Ferry* gives you a great view of the *Statue of Liberty*. But everywhere you look, the buildings and settings feel familiar from movies and TV. The huge open space of *Central Park* is amazing to explore, but the new *High Line Park* on a disused elevated rail line is a unique way to relax above the city streets. With so much to do, it's no wonder the city never sleeps.

POST | CARD

Outside the city, New York has a rich industrial history—the canals that connected the port of New York to the Great Lakes played an important role as the population expanded in the 1830s. *Niagara Falls*, connecting Lake Erie to Lake Ontario, took our breath away. It's not just the scale and sound of the waterfall, but the thousands of rainbows created by the spray.

Nearby, the *Herschell Carrousel Factory Museum* is a must-see.

This factory originally opened in 1915, and now houses exhibits, as well as carousels that can still be ridden. Our ride on one, with hand-carved wooden horses and blaring Wurlitzers, was unforgettable! We then headed for "imaging capital of the world," *Rochester*, where both Kodak and Xerox were founded. All of upstate New York is a surprising contrast to the city, with forests, lakes, and mountains covering the landscape.

Burgers and beers on top of a building in Coney Island.

Inspired by the Statue of Liberty's crown, we've turned one of New York's most famous landmarks into a chic hair accessory that will make you stand out from the crowd.

YOU WILL NEED:

Fourteen ⅜in (10mm) star studs
Five 1½in (40mm) x ¼in (7mm) screwback spikes
Leather
Hairband
Awl
Stud setter
Hot-glue gun
Heavy-duty needle and thread

Liberty Crown Headband

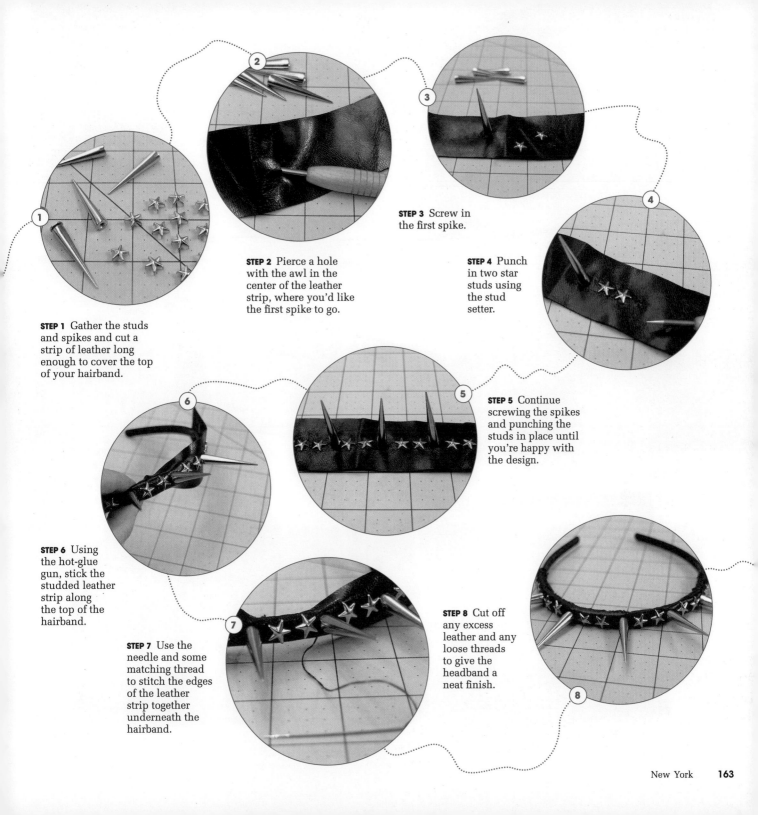

STEP 1 Gather the studs and spikes and cut a strip of leather long enough to cover the top of your hairband.

STEP 2 Pierce a hole with the awl in the center of the leather strip, where you'd like the first spike to go.

STEP 3 Screw in the first spike.

STEP 4 Punch in two star studs using the stud setter.

STEP 5 Continue screwing the spikes and punching the studs in place until you're happy with the design.

STEP 6 Using the hot-glue gun, stick the studded leather strip along the top of the hairband.

STEP 7 Use the needle and some matching thread to stitch the edges of the leather strip together underneath the hairband.

STEP 8 Cut off any excess leather and any loose threads to give the headband a neat finish.

A little snack of deep-fried pickles.

Collecting our winnings from the two-cent machines.

The boardwalk at Seaside Heights.

Crossing the Delaware River into Trenton.

Having a cocktail in Atlantic City.

The seaside theme was everywhere.

Monopoly on the boardwalk, Atlantic City.

New Jersey

Home to more than 1,000 people per square mile, New Jersey is the most densely populated state in the country. With New York City on one side, and Philadelphia on the other, in 1876 Abraham Browning of Camden said that "our Garden State is an immense barrel, filled with good things to eat and open at both ends, with Pennsylvanians grabbing from one end and New Yorkers from the other." The name stuck!

On the coast, *Seaside Heights* is recognizable as the backdrop to MTV's *Jersey Shore*. Though you might not spot any of the stars from the show, there are plenty of Muffler Men advertising sculptures to look out for when walking the boardwalk.

Though we passed through during the off-season, we picked up some fried pickles and headed to the resort of *Atlantic City*, the gambling and casino capital of the East. The first *boardwalk* in the country runs for 4 miles (6.5km) along the beach. Many street names here are familiar from the US Monopoly board! Saltwater taffy, a sticky and chewy candy, is still a popular souvenir from the city.

We were a little too late for the Circus Drive-In.

THANKS FOR A GREAT SEASON

MARYLAND JUMBO SOFT SHELL CRABS

There's a huge amount going on in NJ. Pass some time in the *Silver Ball Pinball Museum* in *Asbury Park*, spot an 8ft (2.5m) replica of Bruce Springsteen's guitar (cnr. E. St. and 10th Ave, *Belmar*), or visit the birthplace of Frank Sinatra in *Hoboken*. You might also recognize a few locations from the movies of Kevin Smith (another local)—they are almost all set here.

Plant-Me Greetings Card

Keep the Garden State in bloom with plantable greetings cards.

YOU WILL NEED:

Picture frame
Mesh (we used sinamay, a hat-making fabric)
String
Yarn needle
Scrap paper (include plenty of color to avoid a gray card)
Flower seeds
Felt square cut to the same size as frame
Blender
Tub that's big enough to hold your frame
Towel

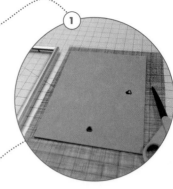

STEP 1 Remove the glass and backing from the frame. Place the backing on top of your mesh and cut the mesh to size, leaving an inch or two around the edges.

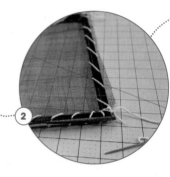

STEP 2 Stitch the mesh to the back of the picture frame using the string and yarn needle.

PLANTING DIRECTIONS

Tear the card up and plant directly into the ground or in a pot. Water in well and don't let the soil dry out.

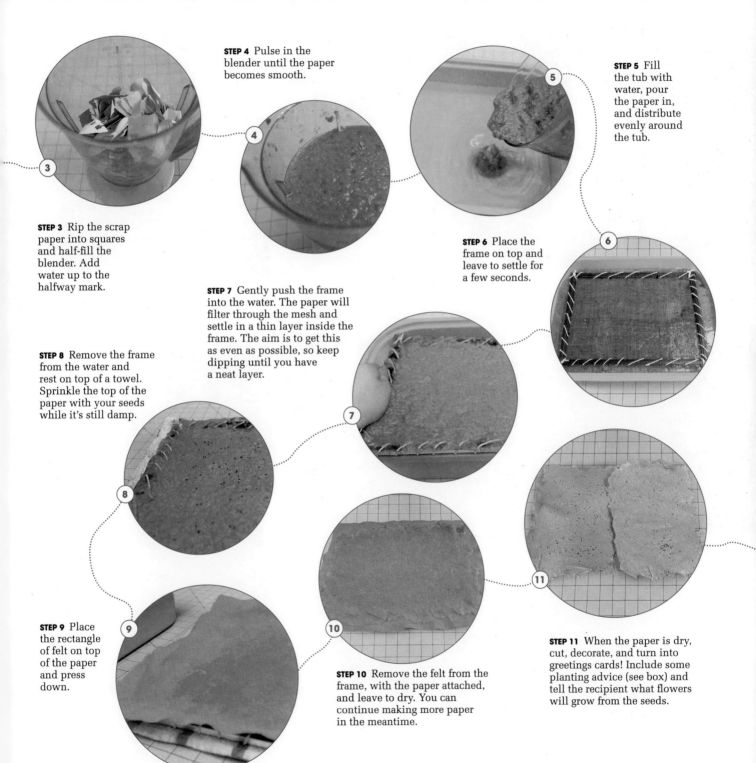

STEP 4 Pulse in the blender until the paper becomes smooth.

STEP 5 Fill the tub with water, pour the paper in, and distribute evenly around the tub.

STEP 3 Rip the scrap paper into squares and half-fill the blender. Add water up to the halfway mark.

STEP 6 Place the frame on top and leave to settle for a few seconds.

STEP 7 Gently push the frame into the water. The paper will filter through the mesh and settle in a thin layer inside the frame. The aim is to get this as even as possible, so keep dipping until you have a neat layer.

STEP 8 Remove the frame from the water and rest on top of a towel. Sprinkle the top of the paper with your seeds while it's still damp.

STEP 9 Place the rectangle of felt on top of the paper and press down.

STEP 10 Remove the felt from the frame, with the paper attached, and leave to dry. You can continue making more paper in the meantime.

STEP 11 When the paper is dry, cut, decorate, and turn into greetings cards! Include some planting advice (see box) and tell the recipient what flowers will grow from the seeds.

Al Capone's luxurious cell in the Eastern State Penitentiary.

The Liberty Bell, Philadelphia.

Making friends at Hershey!

Sunset over the Phillies Baseball Stadium.

Spending the night at the Fulton Steamboat Inn.

Tucking in to vegan Philly cheese steak.

A Coke bottle carved out of a tree.

PENNSYLVANIA

Named after its founder, William Penn, Pennsylvania is known as the State of Independence. Once the capital of the United States, *Philadelphia* is the city where the Declaration of Independence was signed, and tourists flock to see the broken *Liberty Bell* every year. Curious to see how justice was served out in 1829, we took a tour of the *Eastern State Penitentiary (2124 Fairmount Ave.)*, a derelict prison that has recently reopened. Visitors can listen to an audio tour narrated by Steve Buscemi as they explore the eerie passageways and cells. Renovations have concentrated on safety, leaving the peeling paint and rusting doors to add an atmospheric touch. There's even a plush cell where Al Capone stayed as a celebrity inmate, enjoying candlelit dinners!

A trip to the City of Brotherly Love wouldn't be complete without posing on the steps outside the *Philadelphia Museum of Art*, which Sylvester Stallone famously ran up in the *Rocky* movies, and at least one Philly cheese steak. We enjoyed a vegetarian version from *Blackbird Pizzeria (507 S. 6th St.)*.

"The Sweetest Place On Earth," *Hershey* is home to the chocolate factory that churns out Kisses and Peanut Butter Cups all day, every day. We spun round their free factory tour before stocking up on some snacks for the road.

Driving around the state, it's not unusual to see an Amish buggy pulled by a horse. *Lancaster County* holds America's oldest Amish settlement, living a plain lifestyle. We stayed at the *Fulton Steamboat Inn (1 Hartman Bridge Rd.)*, a hotel on land, but designed as a replica steamboat. The steamboat pioneer Robert Fulton was born just a few miles away.

The yard at Eastern State Penitentiary.

Lucky Penny Bracelet

We loved collecting souvenir pennies from all the places we visited on our road trip. Inspired by the United States Mint in Philadelphia, this bracelet is the perfect way to show off your collection without breaking the bank.

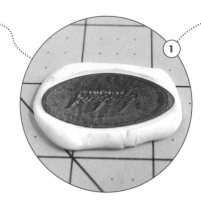

STEP 1 Start by rolling a ball of clay into a flat disk slightly larger than a coin. Press the coin firmly into the clay.

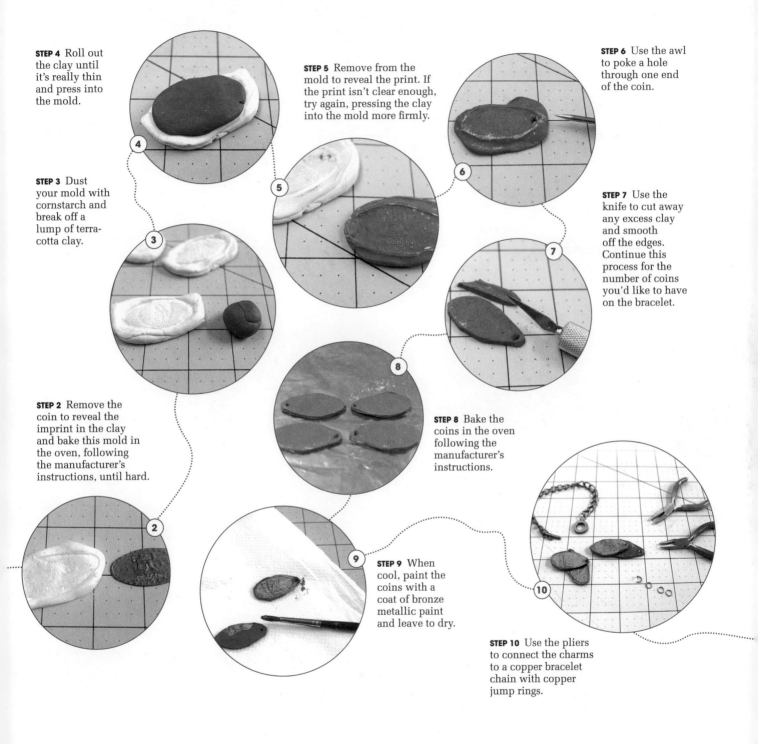

STEP 4 Roll out the clay until it's really thin and press into the mold.

STEP 3 Dust your mold with cornstarch and break off a lump of terracotta clay.

STEP 2 Remove the coin to reveal the imprint in the clay and bake this mold in the oven, following the manufacturer's instructions, until hard.

STEP 5 Remove from the mold to reveal the print. If the print isn't clear enough, try again, pressing the clay into the mold more firmly.

STEP 6 Use the awl to poke a hole through one end of the coin.

STEP 7 Use the knife to cut away any excess clay and smooth off the edges. Continue this process for the number of coins you'd like to have on the bracelet.

STEP 8 Bake the coins in the oven following the manufacturer's instructions.

STEP 9 When cool, paint the coins with a coat of bronze metallic paint and leave to dry.

STEP 10 Use the pliers to connect the charms to a copper bracelet chain with copper jump rings.

Merman taxidermy, Zwaanendael Museum.

The Fountain of Youth, Lewes.

Grabbing lunch at the Dogfish Head
Craft Brewery food truck.

Colorful painted houses, Lewes.

Entering the First City in the First State.

Our lunch—all made with beer, and served with beer!

A steampunk-style treehouse outside the
Dogfish Head Craft Brewery.

Delaware

Despite being the second smallest of the 50 states, Delaware has a huge amount of history. Having been the first to sign the Constitution, it's known as the First State—one plus side of having a small population is that it doesn't take as long for everyone to agree!

Despite familiar English place names such as Dover, Kent, and Sussex, the state was first inhabited by the Dutch. In *Lewes*, the *Zwaanendael Museum* is housed in a replica of a town hall in Holland and is home to the famous but creepy *Delaware Mermaid*. Positioned next to a major shipping channel, Delaware's maritime history tells an amazing story—complete shipwrecks are still discovered preserved in the silt, and you can head to *Coin Beach*, where pennies are regularly washed up.

Though almost a million people live in Delaware, there are more corporations registered here than people. With a pro-business attitude, modern corporate law, and low taxes, more than half of the businesses in the country are incorporated here. Business taxes and fees provide around a quarter of the state budget.

Our first "business trip" was a stop at *Dogfish Head Craft Brewery (6 Cannery Village Center)* in *Milton* for some free samples, and food made with their beer. The brewery has a giant steampunk treehouse outside and offers free tours almost every day. The largest city, *Wilmington*, is at the very north of the state, only 30 miles (50km) from Philadelphia.

A Dutch-themed cross-stitch in the Zwaanendael Museum.

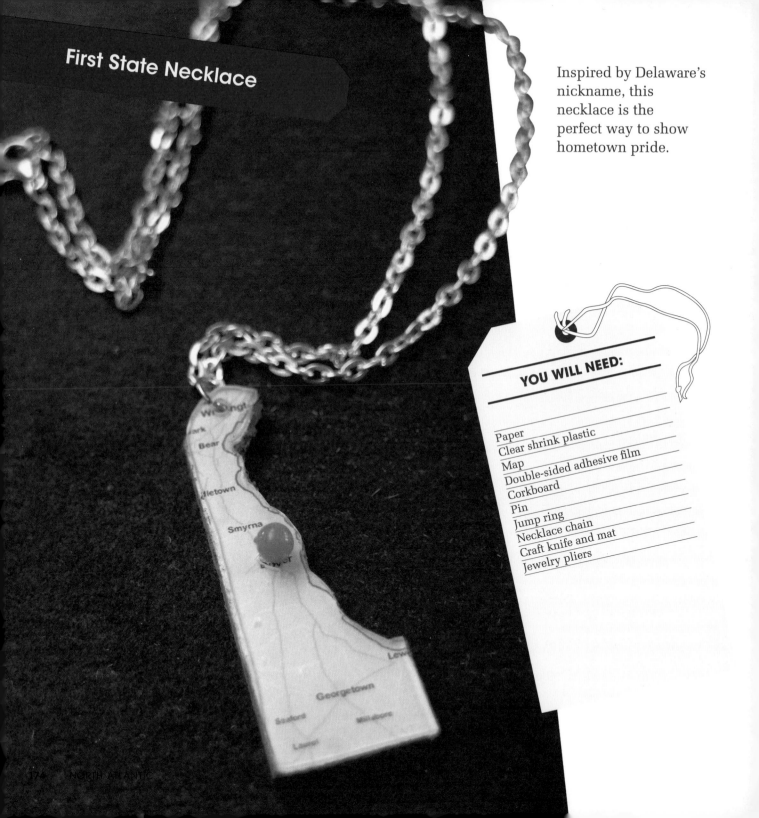

First State Necklace

Inspired by Delaware's nickname, this necklace is the perfect way to show hometown pride.

YOU WILL NEED:

Paper
Clear shrink plastic
Map
Double-sided adhesive film
Corkboard
Pin
Jump ring
Necklace chain
Craft knife and mat
Jewelry pliers

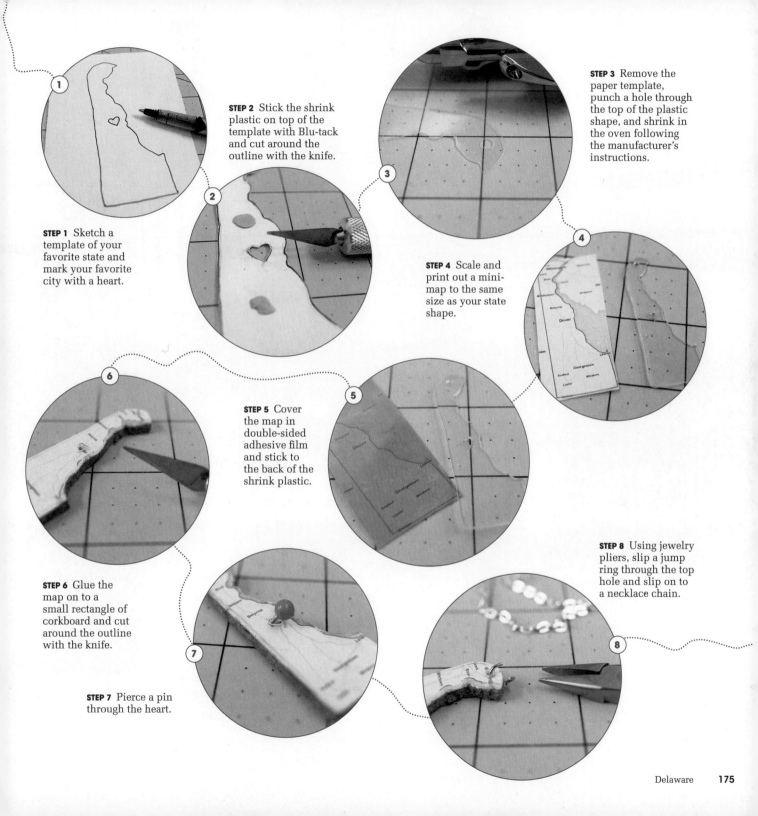

STEP 1 Sketch a template of your favorite state and mark your favorite city with a heart.

STEP 2 Stick the shrink plastic on top of the template with Blu-tack and cut around the outline with the knife.

STEP 3 Remove the paper template, punch a hole through the top of the plastic shape, and shrink in the oven following the manufacturer's instructions.

STEP 4 Scale and print out a mini-map to the same size as your state shape.

STEP 5 Cover the map in double-sided adhesive film and stick to the back of the shrink plastic.

STEP 6 Glue the map on to a small rectangle of corkboard and cut around the outline with the knife.

STEP 7 Pierce a pin through the heart.

STEP 8 Using jewelry pliers, slip a jump ring through the top hole and slip on to a necklace chain.

A view across the Susquehanna River.

Sculpture at the Papermoon Diner.

Sketches at the Baltimore Tattoo Museum.

Pier 5 at Inner Harbor, Baltimore.

Crossing the state line.

Heading into the Baltimore Tattoo Museum.

MARYLAND

Maryland is said to be so jam-packed with things to do, and with such a variety of landscapes, that one of its nicknames is Little America.

The national anthem, "The Star Spangled Banner," is believed to have been written about the flag that flew above the bombardment of Baltimore Harbor in 1814; with each stripe more than 2ft (0.5m) wide, it was definitely "a flag so large that the British would have no difficulty seeing it from a distance." You can visit *The Star-Spangled Banner Flag House* to learn more.

While humming the anthem, we began our *Baltimore* adventure by exploring the picturesque harbor and giggling at the *USS Torsk* submarine, which sits in the bay painted like a shark, ironically close to the *National Aquarium*. A short walk away, we perused the designs and equipment at the *Baltimore Tattoo Museum*, thinking we'd rather stick to needle and thread than needle and ink! If you're a fan of pain, the city is also home to the *National Museum of Dentistry*.

Feeling hungry, we treated ourselves to dinner at the bright and colorful *Papermoon Diner (227 W. 29th St.)* where every inch of wall (and ceiling) is covered in toys, nicknames, and memorabilia.

Steel railway bridges over the Susquehanna.

STEP 1 Use the French curve to draw a swooping collar template measuring roughly 5in (12.5cm) wide by 9in (23cm) long.

Tattoo Sailor Collar

Add a nautical touch to an outfit with this cute sailor collar.

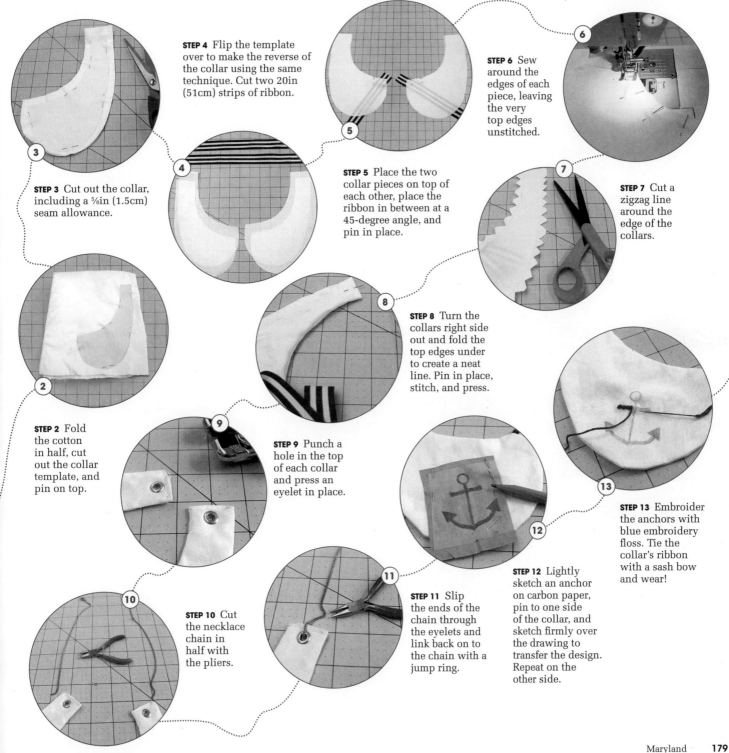

STEP 3 Cut out the collar, including a ⅝in (1.5cm) seam allowance.

STEP 4 Flip the template over to make the reverse of the collar using the same technique. Cut two 20in (51cm) strips of ribbon.

STEP 5 Place the two collar pieces on top of each other, place the ribbon in between at a 45-degree angle, and pin in place.

STEP 6 Sew around the edges of each piece, leaving the very top edges unstitched.

STEP 7 Cut a zigzag line around the edge of the collars.

STEP 8 Turn the collars right side out and fold the top edges under to create a neat line. Pin in place, stitch, and press.

STEP 2 Fold the cotton in half, cut out the collar template, and pin on top.

STEP 9 Punch a hole in the top of each collar and press an eyelet in place.

STEP 10 Cut the necklace chain in half with the pliers.

STEP 11 Slip the ends of the chain through the eyelets and link back on to the chain with a jump ring.

STEP 12 Lightly sketch an anchor on carbon paper, pin to one side of the collar, and sketch firmly over the drawing to transfer the design. Repeat on the other side.

STEP 13 Embroider the anchors with blue embroidery floss. Tie the collar's ribbon with a sash bow and wear!

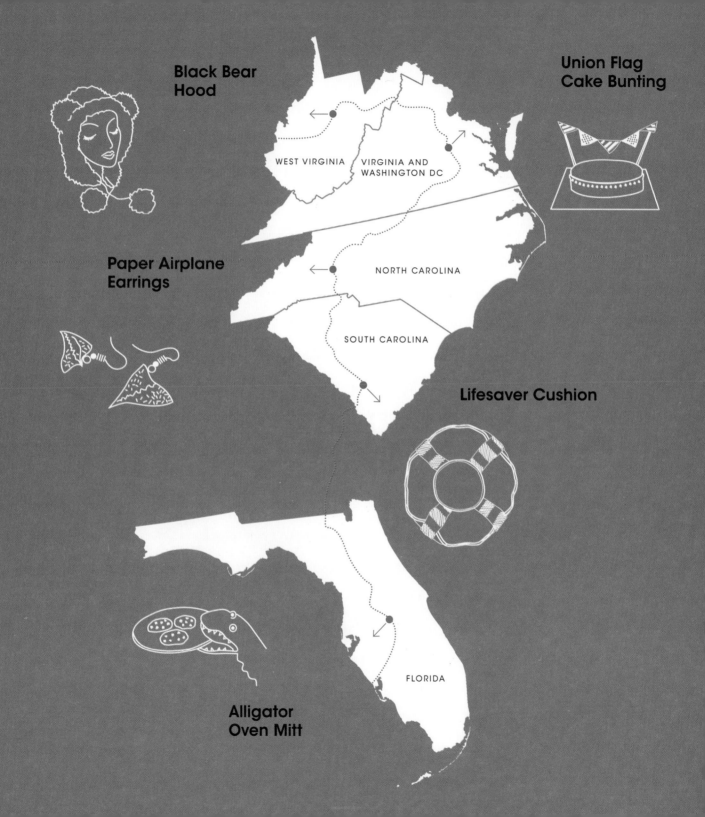

Black Bear Hood

Union Flag Cake Bunting

Paper Airplane Earrings

WEST VIRGINIA

VIRGINIA AND WASHINGTON DC

NORTH CAROLINA

SOUTH CAROLINA

Lifesaver Cushion

FLORIDA

Alligator Oven Mitt

SOUTH ATLANTIC

Heading down the trail to the
New River Gorge Bridge.

The Haunted Cottage, Harpers Ferry.

Don't let a tractor ruin your
trip—you have been warned!

A civil war cannon at Droop Mountain
Battlefield State Park.

Hillybilly Hot Dogs.

Driving through Charles Town
in the east of the state.

Our first stop—the welcome center.

West Virginia

Tucked away in the Appalachian Mountains, West Virginia is a huge contrast to the cities and bustle of the east coast. The iconic *New River Gorge Bridge*, pictured on the state quarter coin, takes you over an 876ft (267m) drop, and an incredible view across rich forests.

We took the Highland Scenic Parkway to *Beartown State Park*, near *Hillsboro*, where the state animal, the black bear, likes to spend winters in the caves and unusual rocks. A boardwalk around the park gives a great view down into the wilderness.

West Virginia was formed during the Civil War, and the important battleground at nearby *Droop Mountain* is just one of the places to learn about the history, with full-scale battle re-enactments every two years.

Over at *Hillbilly Hot Dogs (6951 Ohio River Rd., Lesage)*, they take the redneck stereotype seriously and serve hot dogs from a shack filled with jokes and slang. Give them a tip, and they'll sing their "We've Got the Weenies" song!

At *Harpers Ferry* in the eastern panhandle of the state, the Potomac and Shenandoah rivers merge at the state line between Maryland and Virginia, where John Brown raided the Armory in an attempt to start a slave liberation movement in 1859. Although Brown was unsuccessful, the 13th Amendment later ended slavery in 1865.

For some more recent history, the secret underground bunker at *The Greenbrier (300 W. Main St.)* in *White Sulphur Springs* would have housed the members of Congress in 5ft (1.5m)-thick walls during a Cold War emergency. Nowadays, you can take a tour of the facility.

Welcome To WEST VIRGINIA — Wild and Wonderful

Black bears know how to stay warm in winter. We're sharing some of their secrets with this hood!

Black Bear Hood

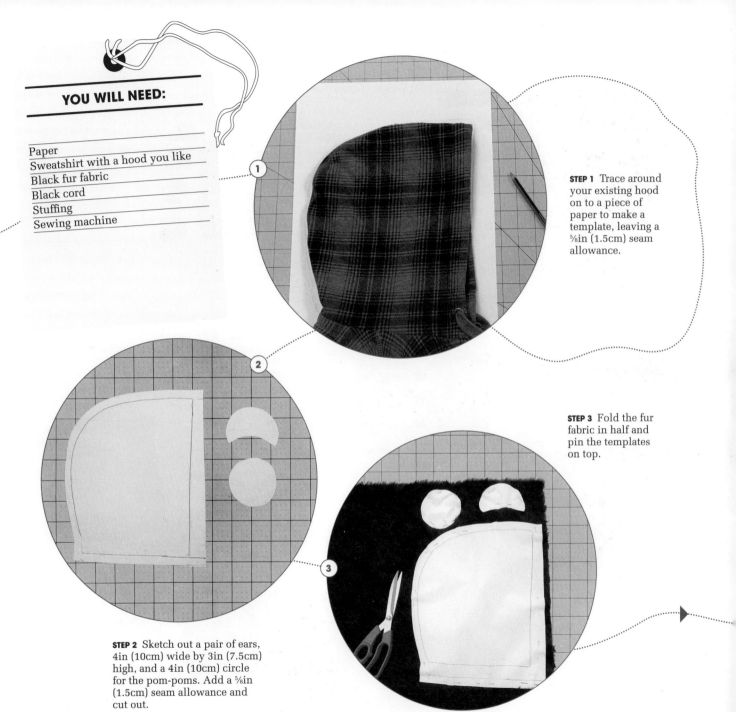

YOU WILL NEED:

Paper
Sweatshirt with a hood you like
Black fur fabric
Black cord
Stuffing
Sewing machine

STEP 1 Trace around your existing hood on to a piece of paper to make a template, leaving a ⅝in (1.5cm) seam allowance.

STEP 3 Fold the fur fabric in half and pin the templates on top.

STEP 2 Sketch out a pair of ears, 4in (10cm) wide by 3in (7.5cm) high, and a 4in (10cm) circle for the pom-poms. Add a ⅝in (1.5cm) seam allowance and cut out.

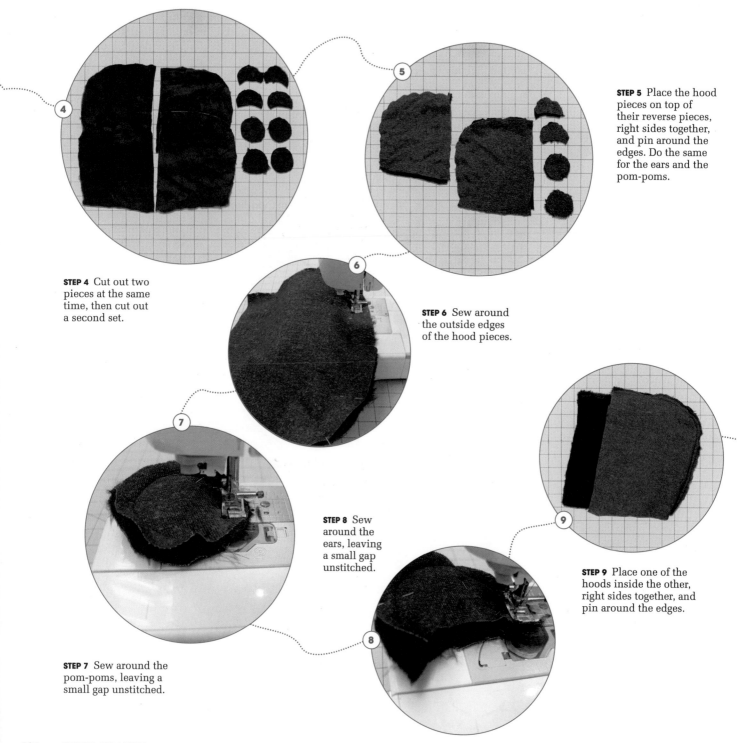

STEP 4 Cut out two pieces at the same time, then cut out a second set.

STEP 5 Place the hood pieces on top of their reverse pieces, right sides together, and pin around the edges. Do the same for the ears and the pom-poms.

STEP 6 Sew around the outside edges of the hood pieces.

STEP 7 Sew around the pom-poms, leaving a small gap unstitched.

STEP 8 Sew around the ears, leaving a small gap unstitched.

STEP 9 Place one of the hoods inside the other, right sides together, and pin around the edges.

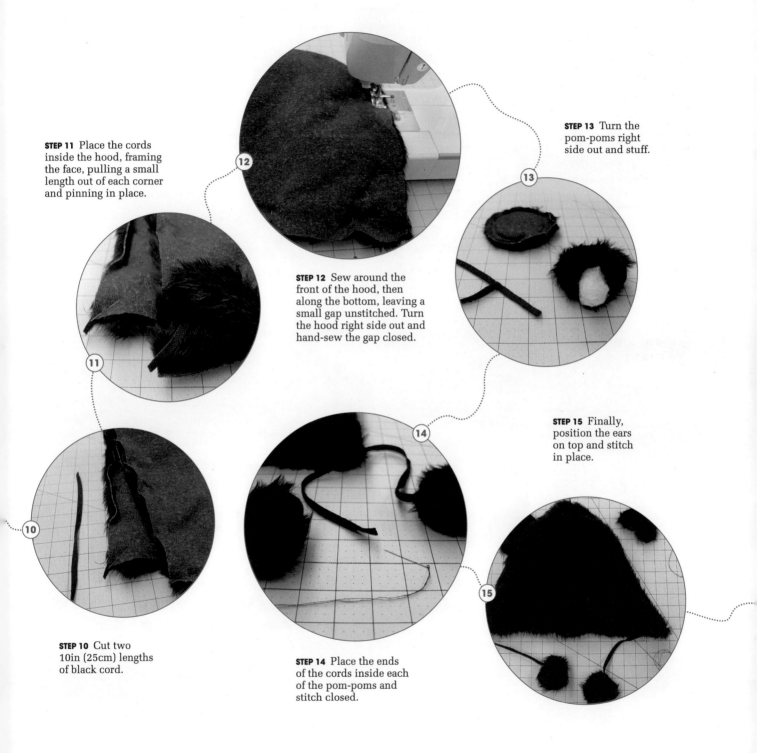

STEP 11 Place the cords inside the hood, framing the face, pulling a small length out of each corner and pinning in place.

STEP 12 Sew around the front of the hood, then along the bottom, leaving a small gap unstitched. Turn the hood right side out and hand-sew the gap closed.

STEP 13 Turn the pom-poms right side out and stuff.

STEP 15 Finally, position the ears on top and stitch in place.

STEP 10 Cut two 10in (25cm) lengths of black cord.

STEP 14 Place the ends of the cords inside each of the pom-poms and stitch closed.

West Virginia **187**

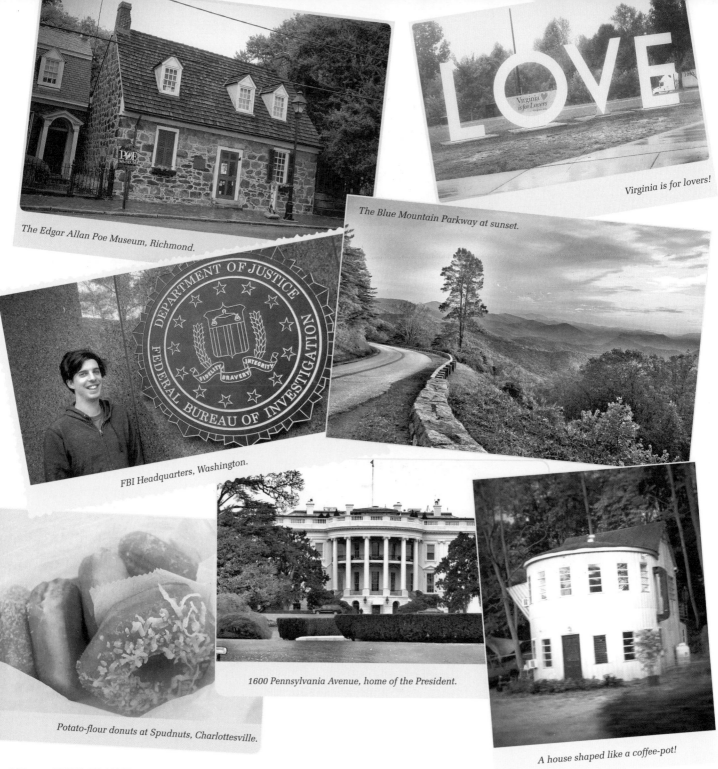

The Edgar Allan Poe Museum, Richmond.

Virginia is for lovers!

The Blue Mountain Parkway at sunset.

FBI Headquarters, Washington.

Potato-flour donuts at Spudnuts, Charlottesville.

1600 Pennsylvania Avenue, home of the President.

A house shaped like a coffee-pot!

Virginia and Washington DC

Being the birthplace of eight presidents, and bordering the capital city, it's no wonder politics have played a huge role in defining Virginia.

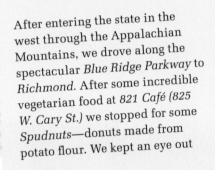

After entering the state in the west through the Appalachian Mountains, we drove along the spectacular *Blue Ridge Parkway* to *Richmond*. After some incredible vegetarian food at *821 Café (825 W. Cary St.)* we stopped for some *Spudnuts*—donuts made from potato flour. We kept an eye out for the state bird, the cardinal, which is bright crimson. Edgar Allan Poe grew up in the city, and his work is preserved in the oldest building in the city, now the *Poe Museum*. Alternatively, check out his dorm room at the *University of Virginia*.

POST CARD

Though we didn't get a chance to see the grave (and false teeth!) of George Washington at *Mount Vernon*, we made sure to visit *Washington, D.C.*, just across the Potomac River. After posing with the *White House*, the *US Capitol*, and the *FBI Headquarters*, we went to see the amazing space of *Union Station*. Across the US we saw many commemorative flags once flown at the Capitol—more than 100,000 different flags fly there during each year, after requests from the public.

Back in Virginia, at the naval base of *Cape Henry*, you can visit the site of the first landing of the British in the US in 1607, across from the first US lighthouse. Leaving the state, we crossed the 23 mile (37km)-long *Chesapeake Bay Bridge-Tunnel*, an amazing collection of bridges, tunnels, and artificial islands leading to Cape Charles.

The second lighthouse at Cape Henry, next to the First Landing point.

Union Flag Cake Bunting

Washington's birthday is celebrated as President's Day across the country. Why not stitch up some cute bunting to make an extra-special treat?

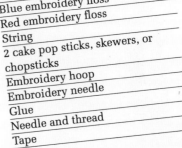

YOU WILL NEED:

White cross-stitch fabric/ Aida cloth

Blue embroidery floss

Red embroidery floss

String

2 cake pop sticks, skewers, or chopsticks

Embroidery hoop

Embroidery needle

Glue

Needle and thread

Tape

Charts:

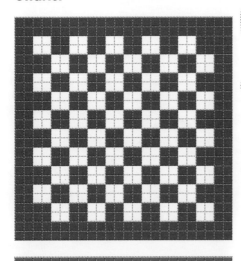

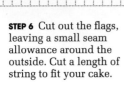

STEP 1 Secure the Aida cloth inside the embroidery hoop and thread the needle with blue floss, tying a knot at one end. Bring the needle through the fabric from the back.

STEP 2 Make your first (diagonal) stitch by putting the needle through the hole one to the right and one down.

STEP 3 Following the chart horizontally, continue making diagonal stitches along the top. When you reach the end of the row (24 stitches), reverse the direction of your stitches, turning your initial stitches into crosses.

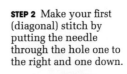

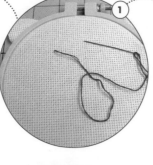

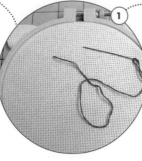

STEP 4 When you come to a gap in the pattern, simply bring the needle up several holes along, leaving the correct number of unstitched squares.

STEP 5 Continue stitching until you reach the end of the chart and then tie a knot on the reverse of your work. Make one more star flag and three striped flags.

STEP 6 Cut out the flags, leaving a small seam allowance around the outside. Cut a length of string to fit your cake.

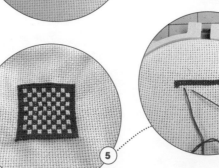

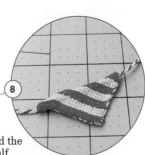

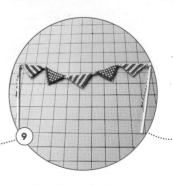

STEP 8 Fold the flags in half diagonally, place over the string, and stitch in place.

STEP 9 Tape the ends of the string to the sticks and adorn your cake!

STEP 7 Fold a neat edge around the flags and use a small amount of glue to stick in place at the back.

The Wright brothers' plane, now at the Henry Ford Museum, Detroit.

Driving through the scenic Smoky Mountains.

Pigs in Pack Square, along the Asheville Urban Trail.

Stopping for a vegan pulled pork burger at the Remedy Diner in Raleigh.

David Cerny's Metalmorphosis sculpture in Charlotte.

Stopping at a roadside shack for boiled peanuts.

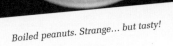

Boiled peanuts. Strange… but tasty!

NORTH CAROLINA

Known as the Old North State, North Carolina is famous for the *Smoky Mountains*, being the BBQ capital of the world, and the first flight made by the Wright brothers in Kitty Hawk in 1903.

Starting at the coast and beaches of *Wilmington*, we made tracks to the state capital, *Raleigh*. Don't worry if you're more of an animal lover than a meat eater because you can get a taste of BBQ at *The Remedy Diner (137 E. Hargett St.)*, where they serve up delicious vegan versions of the state's famous cuisine, such as pulled pork and the Reuben. Strike your best superhero pose at the nearby *Nature Research Center*, where they have a giant Earth statue, similar to the one from the *Daily Planet* in *Superman*.

We stopped off at the largest city, *Charlotte*, to see *Metalmorphosis*, a 22ft (7m)-tall head sculpture that spits out water into a fountain. Back on the road, we took a picturesque drive through the *Great Smoky Mountains*, past *Mount Mitchell*, the highest peak on the East Coast, and stopped at a roadside shack to buy some fresh boiled peanuts. The colors, forests, and views are spectacular, especially at sunset, when the light catches the leaves.

We then made our way to the hipster city of *Asheville*, which is full of cool coffee shops, street art, and independent boutiques. Keep an eye out for nuns on bikes as you wander around the city (we spotted two!), and if you're lucky you might even get to join a drumming circle in the center of town. We tucked into healthy salads at the *Green Sage Coffeehouse and Café*

(5 Broadway), but if you're looking for something a little different, stop off at *Double D's (41 Biltmore Ave.)*, an old double-decker bus turned coffee shop. You'd need a full day or more to explore the 250 rooms of the *Biltmore Estate*, the largest private residence in the US, built by George Vanderbilt in 1889.

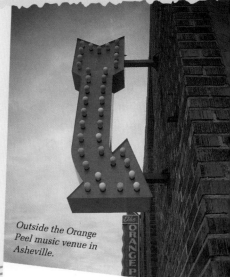

Outside the Orange Peel music venue in Asheville.

Inspired by the Wright brothers' first flight in North Carolina, you'll feel like a high flyer wearing these silver charm earrings.

YOU WILL NEED:

Paper
Silver clay
Jump rings
Earring hooks
Mini rolling pin
Craft knife
Awl
Brick
Blowtorch
Toothbrush
Jewelry pliers

Paper Airplane Earrings

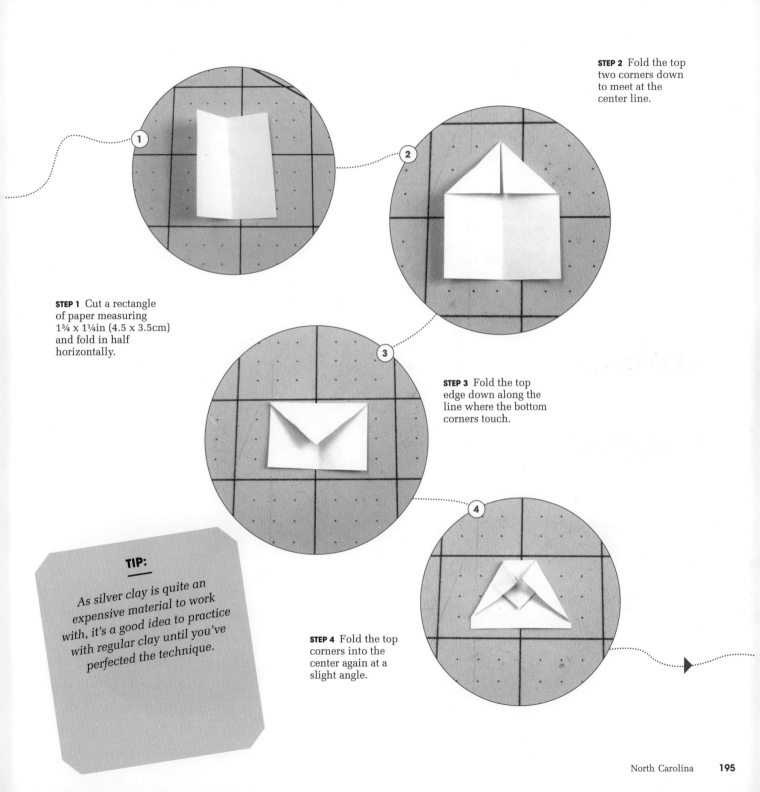

STEP 2 Fold the top two corners down to meet at the center line.

STEP 1 Cut a rectangle of paper measuring 1¾ x 1¼in (4.5 x 3.5cm) and fold in half horizontally.

STEP 3 Fold the top edge down along the line where the bottom corners touch.

TIP:

As silver clay is quite an expensive material to work with, it's a good idea to practice with regular clay until you've perfected the technique.

STEP 4 Fold the top corners into the center again at a slight angle.

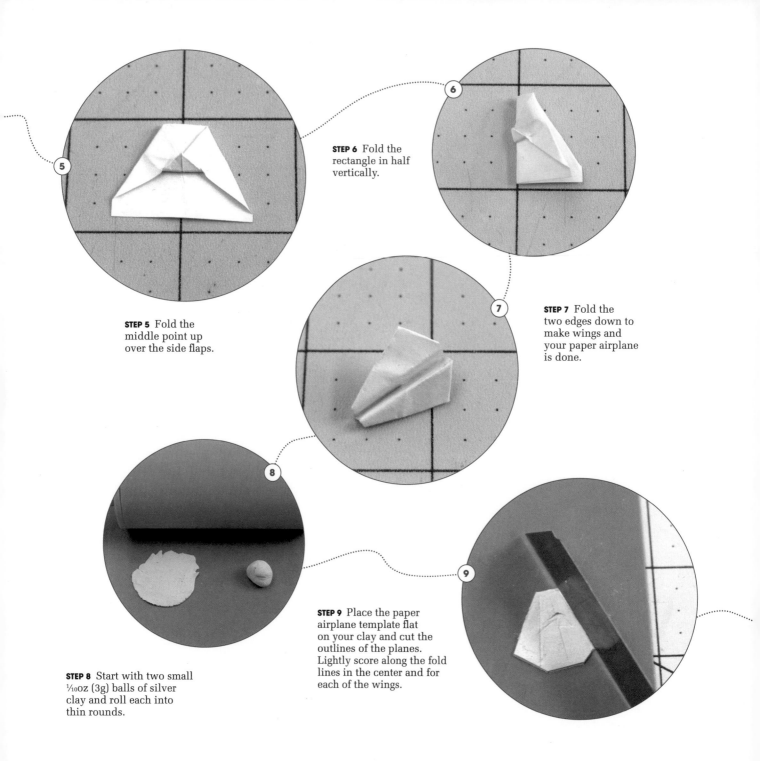

STEP 5 Fold the middle point up over the side flaps.

STEP 6 Fold the rectangle in half vertically.

STEP 7 Fold the two edges down to make wings and your paper airplane is done.

STEP 8 Start with two small ¹⁄₁₀oz (3g) balls of silver clay and roll each into thin rounds.

STEP 9 Place the paper airplane template flat on your clay and cut the outlines of the planes. Lightly score along the fold lines in the center and for each of the wings.

STEP 11 When you're happy with your design, place each clay earring on top of the brick and fire the metal with the blowtorch.

STEP 12 Stop firing when the entire plane begins to glow bright red, or you will melt your design. If parts of the earring are still soft, fire for a few more seconds until they harden into silver.

STEP 13 Polish the earring with a toothbrush to make it shine.

STEP 10 Squeeze together the clay planes in the middle and flatten out the wings. Use the awl to pierce a hole in each earring.

STEP 14 Using jewelry pliers, slip a jump ring through the hole in the wing and attach your planes to earring hooks.

The big wheel on Myrtle Beach.

The UFO Welcome Center, Bowman.

Chain art connecting buildings in Columbia.

Beachfront houses in Myrtle Beach.

Cape Romain Wildlife Refuge was full of cranes.

The World's Largest Fire Hydrant, Columbia.

A baseball-shaped water tower, Fort Mill.

SOUTH CAROLINA

The beautiful trees that line its beaches give this state its nickname—the Palmetto State. As you enter South Carolina, the laid-back attitude of the South starts to creep in, inviting you to spend a day lazing on the beach or in one of the amazing state parks. We began our adventure in the historic city of *Charlotte*, where beautiful white-pillared houses overlook white sandy beaches. We stopped for breakfast at *WildFlour Pastry (73 Spring St.)* before going bird spotting at the *Cape Romain National Wildlife Refuge*.

Although we saw all kinds of Welcome Centers throughout our trip, nothing compared to the *UFO Welcome Center* we passed by in *Bowman*. Built in one man's backyard, this gigantic wood, steel, and fiberglass structure has been constructed to greet aliens after their long trip to Earth. So far, it's only welcomed humans, but we're sure extraterrestrials will appreciate the gesture!

Farther up the coast in *Myrtle Beach* the vibe is a bit more upbeat, with busy souvenir stores, and hotel towers that bring 14 million visitors to the huge beaches and abundant sunshine every year.

Over in the capital, *Columbia*, we loved all the art and sculptures dotted around the center. A giant fire hydrant, chains connecting buildings, and stunning murals meant there was a lot to look at. Another must-see is *Congaree National Park*, where tall hardwood trees grow out of the floodland swamps.

Cape Romain
NATIONAL WILDLIFE REFUGE

U.S. Fish and Wildlife Service
Department of the Interior

We loved seeing all the birds at Cape Romain!

Lifesaver Cushion

Inspired by Myrtle Beach, this nautical pillow will bring a touch of the seaside to your home and "save" you from discomfort.

YOU WILL NEED:

- Muslin (calico)
- Striped fabric
- Stuffing
- String or thin rope
- Sewing machine
- Needle and thread
- Seam ripper

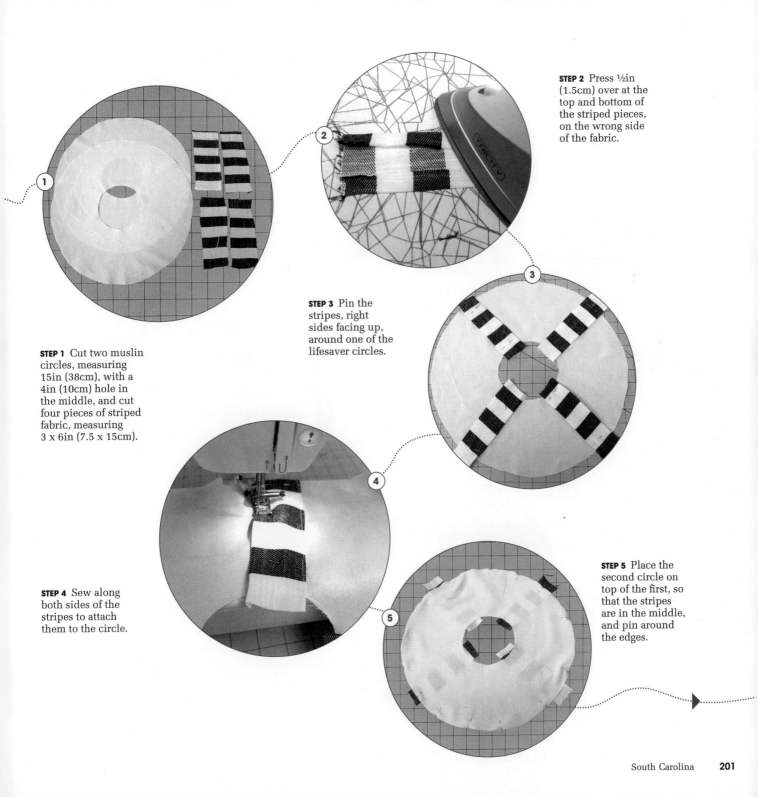

STEP 2 Press ½in (1.5cm) over at the top and bottom of the striped pieces, on the wrong side of the fabric.

STEP 3 Pin the stripes, right sides facing up, around one of the lifesaver circles.

STEP 1 Cut two muslin circles, measuring 15in (38cm), with a 4in (10cm) hole in the middle, and cut four pieces of striped fabric, measuring 3 x 6in (7.5 x 15cm).

STEP 4 Sew along both sides of the stripes to attach them to the circle.

STEP 5 Place the second circle on top of the first, so that the stripes are in the middle, and pin around the edges.

South Carolina   **201**

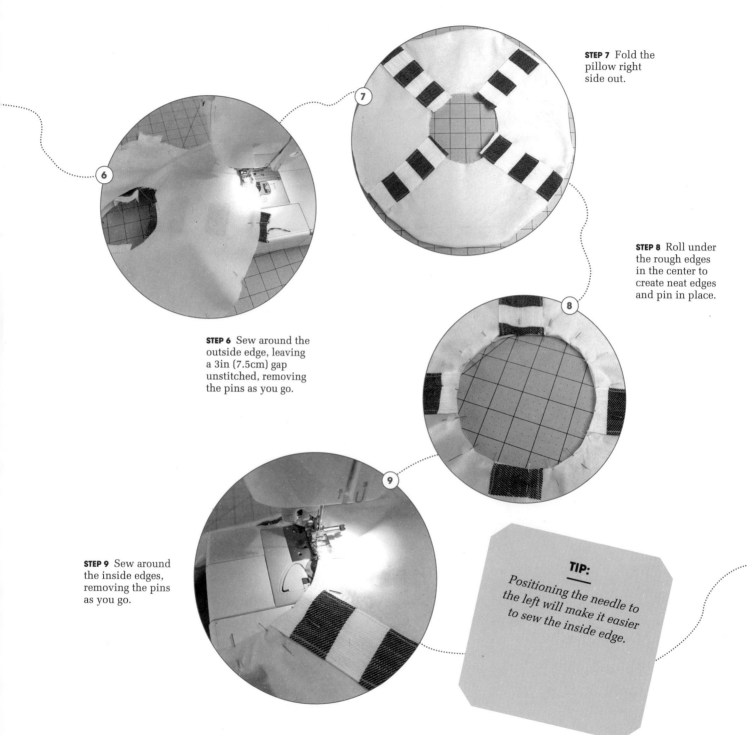

STEP 7 Fold the pillow right side out.

STEP 8 Roll under the rough edges in the center to create neat edges and pin in place.

STEP 6 Sew around the outside edge, leaving a 3in (7.5cm) gap unstitched, removing the pins as you go.

STEP 9 Sew around the inside edges, removing the pins as you go.

TIP:

Positioning the needle to the left will make it easier to sew the inside edge.

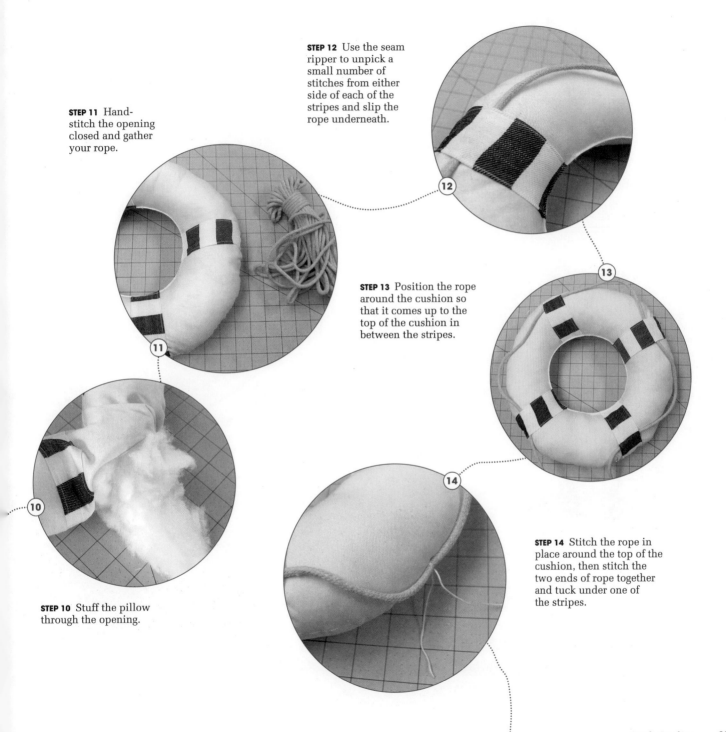

STEP 12 Use the seam ripper to unpick a small number of stitches from either side of each of the stripes and slip the rope underneath.

STEP 11 Hand-stitch the opening closed and gather your rope.

STEP 13 Position the rope around the cushion so that it comes up to the top of the cushion in between the stripes.

STEP 10 Stuff the pillow through the opening.

STEP 14 Stitch the rope in place around the top of the cushion, then stitch the two ends of rope together and tuck under one of the stripes.

Crossing the Garcon Point Bridge near Pensacola.

Colorful crossings at 5 Points in Jacksonville.

A Florida sandhill crane poses for a photo.

NASA space suit at the Welcome Center on I-5.

Alligator basking in the sun.

Looking across the Gulf of Mexico.

Cotton fields along the highway.

FLORIDA

With free orange juice on offer at its Welcome Center, it feels like you're on vacation as soon as you enter the state of Florida. Home to NASA, beaches, and dozens of theme parks, it's no wonder that thousands of college freshmen make their way here for Spring Break.

The city of *Orlando* in the middle of the state attracts visitors to its world-famous theme parks, and the *Florida Keys* are a string of beautiful islands in the south. Florida's a big place, and our itinerary didn't allow quite enough time to make it all the way round—we'd love to come back and visit the Art Deco seafront of *Miami*, and meet some of the local wildlife in the *Everglades*.

If you're feeling brave, you can drive along one of the beaches on the east coast, although we only made it about a foot off the path before our tire got stuck and we had to be rescued by a muscular passerby.

POST | CARD

The Sunshine State isn't just for students; with its stunning beaches and sparkling oceans, it's easy to see why so many people choose to retire here. Retirees aren't the only ones to migrate here, either—we spotted lots of birds similar to the ones in Hawaii, from stunning white cranes to bright red cardinals. If you're more interested in bigger, scarier animals, a swamp tour is the perfect wildlife thrill ride.

We met a giant alligator for ourselves in *Jacksonville* while exploring the city. Then, after a round of bingo while waiting for our pizza at *Mellow Mushroom (275 Dogwood Blvd., Flowood, MS)*, we began to make our way north up the highway.

Giant alligator in Jacksonville.

Alligator Oven Mitt

They say the NASA landing strip at Kennedy Space Center is the longest alligator sunbathing strip in the world. This gator'll stop you getting singed by the oven.

YOU WILL NEED:

Paper
Green tweed
Red heat-resistant batting (wadding)
Safety eyes
White felt
Sewing machine

STEP 1 Trace around your hand on a piece of paper to create a mitt shape, measuring roughly 8 x 13in (20 x 33cm).

STEP 4 Place the two tweed mitt pieces on top of the two wadding mitt pieces, right sides together, and pin around the edges. Place two mitt top pieces on top of the remaining mitt tops, right sides together, and pin around the edges.

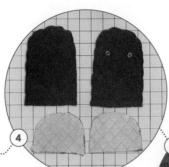

STEP 6 Cut a zigzag edge around each piece to prevent fraying.

STEP 5 Sew around the edges, leaving a small gap on each unstitched so you can turn them inside out. Remove the pins as you go.

STEP 3 Mark the position for the eyes with pins on one mitt shape, pierce the fabric, and slip the eyes into place.

STEP 8 Stitch along both of these lines, removing the pins as you go.

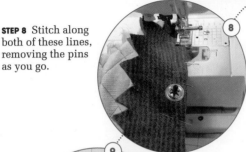

STEP 7 Pinch two lines along either side of the alligator's face to mark its nostrils and pin in place.

STEP 12 Sew around the outside of the oven mitt, leaving the bottom edge unstitched for your hand.

STEP 9 Make a set of jagged teeth by cutting a zigzag line along two 9 x 2in (23 x 5cm) rectangles of white felt.

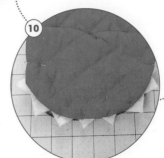

STEP 11 Place the two mitt tops on top of each other, pin in place, and sew together.

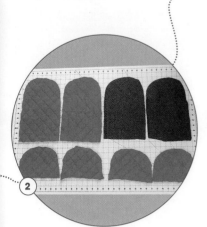

STEP 2 Cut two mitt shapes from the tweed, two from the wadding, and four mitt tops that are roughly 6in (18cm) long.

STEP 10 Place the mitt tops on top of the mitts, with the bottom facing up, and sandwich the teeth in between, pinning around the edges.

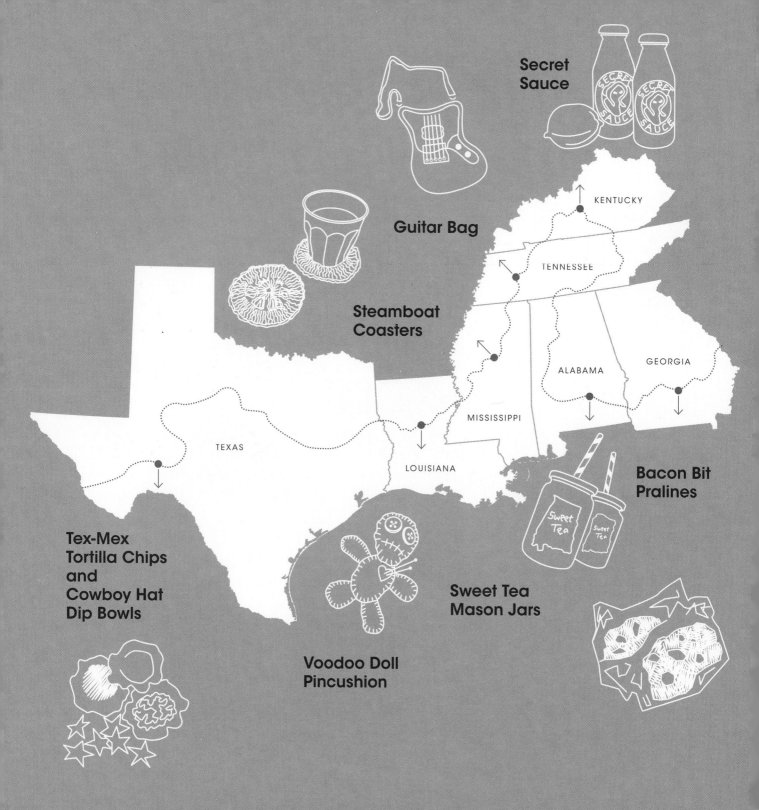

Secret Sauce

Guitar Bag

Steamboat Coasters

KENTUCKY

TENNESSEE

GEORGIA

ALABAMA

MISSISSIPPI

Bacon Bit Pralines

TEXAS

LOUISIANA

Tex-Mex
Tortilla Chips
and
Cowboy Hat
Dip Bowls

Sweet Tea
Mason Jars

Voodoo Doll
Pincushion

A bull at the Fort Worth Stockyards.

The Cathedral of Junk, Austin.

A ranch entrance with delicate ironwork.

Bat sculpture at Congress Avenue Bridge in Austin, just before the bats came out!

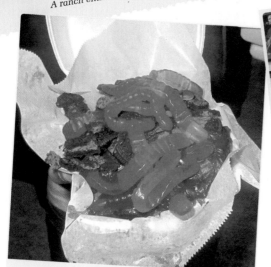

Donut covered in Oreo cookies and gummy worms from Gourdough's food truck.

RAD, the 1980s border patrol robot at the National Border Patrol Museum, El Paso.

One of many giant arrow sculptures across the Quanah Parker Trail in western Texas.

Texas

The Dallas skyline from Trinity Overlook Park.

Everything's bigger in Texas, and after a *whole day* driving through the desert, we believe it! Luckily the state has the highest speed limit in the country to help shave off some time as you cross it. With a unique history and culture, the Texan way of life is bold, brash, and confident.

Dallas and *Fort Worth* are distinct cities with centers 30 miles (48km) apart, but as each has sprawled outward, they have merged to form the largest metropolitan area in the South, with around six million inhabitants. With thousands of miles of highway, and more malls per capita than anywhere else, you'd think that driving all day between the stores would be the thing to do. But downtown Dallas has a lot to offer.

After joining the cowboys and 70 cast-iron bulls for a photo at *Pioneer Plaza* and the iconic *City Hall*, we drove past the *Texas School Book Depository*. (Of course, John F. Kennedy's trip to Dallas ended in tragedy here, and the area is filled with visitors every day.) The arts district is full of galleries and theaters, all housed in incredible architecture. Then, over in Fort Worth, the *Stockyards* showed us the life of a cowboy. Although definitely a draw for the tourists, nothing beats the rodeo atmosphere and cowtown vibes.

Farther south in the capital, *Austin*, the attitude couldn't be more different. Hip bars spring up almost overnight, alongside trendy food trucks and indie music festivals.

It's no wonder that thousands of bats choose the *Congress Avenue Bridge* on their migratory route, and fly out en masse after sunset. We visited the *Alamo Drafthouse (The Ritz, 320 E. 6th St.)*, a movie theater with local beer and meals served during the movie, and Sandra Bullock's *Walton's Fancy and Staple (609 W. 6th St.)*. In a local backyard, we witnessed the *Cathedral of Junk (4422 Lareina Dr.)*, a three-story collection of spaces built with 60 tons of recycled *everything*. Getting hungry, we stopped by *Gourdough's (1503 S. 1st St.)* for a gummy worm and Oreo-topped donut. Delicious!

Rural Texas is scattered with ranches and oil derricks, but the city of *El Paso* was a great stop, with its strong Hispanic flavor and small cantinas everywhere. The Rio Grande separates the city from the (much larger) Mexican city of Juarez—at night the division was clear, as the streetlights glowed from across the border, and the *National Border Patrol Museum* taught us about the ever-changing role of policing it.

For Texans, the most important stop is *The Alamo* in *San Antonio*, where the independence of the Republic of Texas was defended by Davy Crockett, William Barrett Travis, and James Bowie. Today, the fairy-lit canals of the city are perfect for an evening stroll or meal.

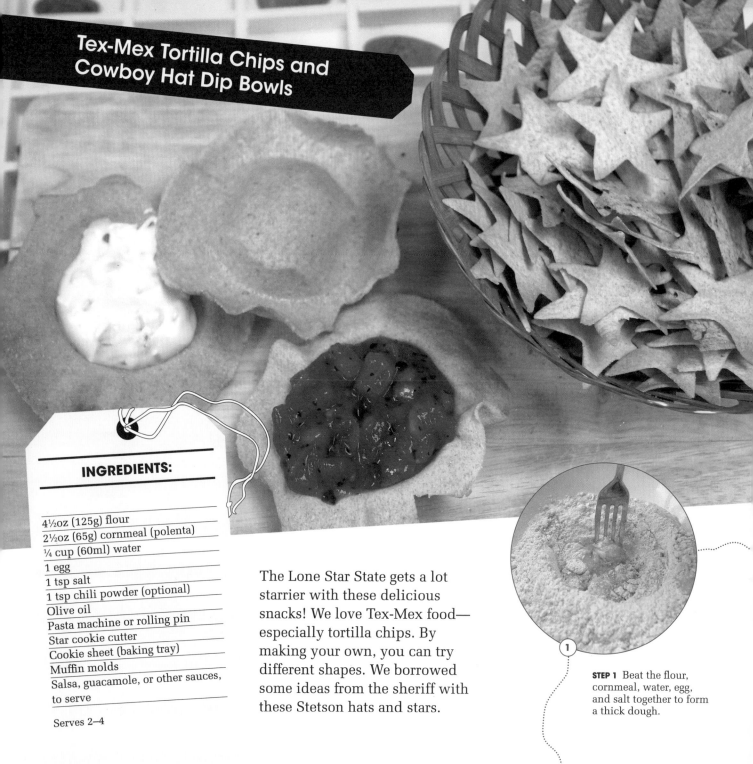

Tex-Mex Tortilla Chips and Cowboy Hat Dip Bowls

INGREDIENTS:

4½oz (125g) flour
2½oz (65g) cornmeal (polenta)
¼ cup (60ml) water
1 egg
1 tsp salt
1 tsp chili powder (optional)
Olive oil
Pasta machine or rolling pin
Star cookie cutter
Cookie sheet (baking tray)
Muffin molds
Salsa, guacamole, or other sauces, to serve

Serves 2–4

The Lone Star State gets a lot starrier with these delicious snacks! We love Tex-Mex food—especially tortilla chips. By making your own, you can try different shapes. We borrowed some ideas from the sheriff with these Stetson hats and stars.

STEP 1 Beat the flour, cornmeal, water, egg, and salt together to form a thick dough.

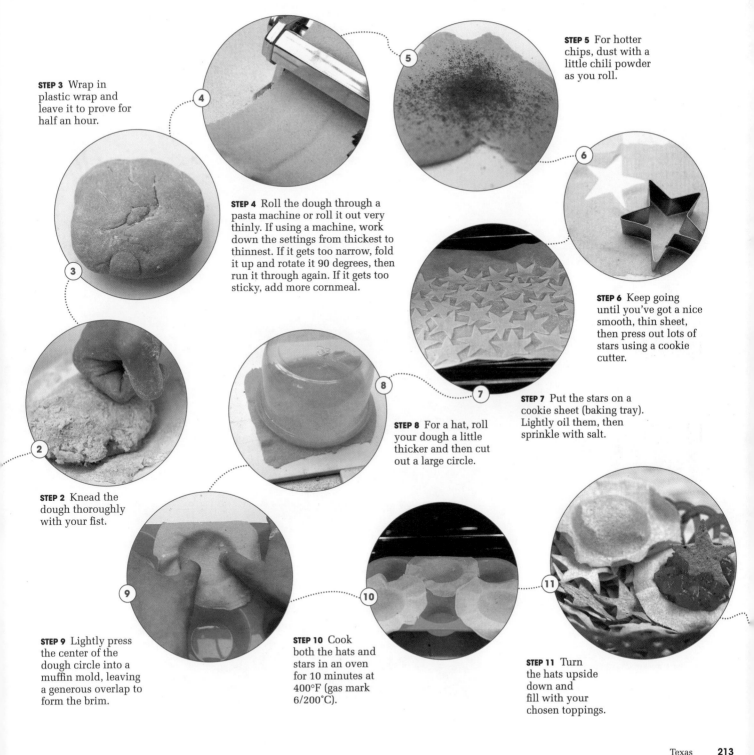

STEP 3 Wrap in plastic wrap and leave it to prove for half an hour.

STEP 4 Roll the dough through a pasta machine or roll it out very thinly. If using a machine, work down the settings from thickest to thinnest. If it gets too narrow, fold it up and rotate it 90 degrees, then run it through again. If it gets too sticky, add more cornmeal.

STEP 5 For hotter chips, dust with a little chili powder as you roll.

STEP 6 Keep going until you've got a nice smooth, thin sheet, then press out lots of stars using a cookie cutter.

STEP 7 Put the stars on a cookie sheet (baking tray). Lightly oil them, then sprinkle with salt.

STEP 8 For a hat, roll your dough a little thicker and then cut out a large circle.

STEP 2 Knead the dough thoroughly with your fist.

STEP 9 Lightly press the center of the dough circle into a muffin mold, leaving a generous overlap to form the brim.

STEP 10 Cook both the hats and stars in an oven for 10 minutes at 400°F (gas mark 6/200°C).

STEP 11 Turn the hats upside down and fill with your chosen toppings.

Hot gumbo at the Gumbo Shop, New Orleans.

Wildlife spotting among the cypresses at Black Bayou Lake National Wildlife Refuge.

Mardi Gras art, New Orleans.

Lafayette Cemetery, one of many around New Orleans.

Spending the night in a cabin on a swamp at the Wildlife Gardens.

An albino alligator at the Wildlife Gardens.

Beignets (and lots of icing sugar) at Café Du Monde, New Orleans.

LOUISIANA

Made up of parishes instead of counties, Louisiana was originally settled by the French, and you can witness this in its architecture, cuisine, and amazing accent. As most of the land was formed from mud washed down the Mississippi River, the state is covered in swamps, bayous, marshes, and wetlands. Combined with a subtropical climate, these make it the perfect environment for birds, frogs, and, of course, alligators. We couldn't help but giggle at the Welcome Center's "No swimming" signs, followed by "Beware of alligators" warnings!

With the promise of being able to feed some 'gators from our porch, we checked into a cabin on the swamp at the *Wildlife Gardens* in *Thibodaux*: Bed and breakfast meets nature park. We spent a slightly terrifying night listening to chirruping insects and critters crawling across our roof—luckily our host saved her stories about Rougarou (a mythical forest creature who can turn you to stone) until breakfast the next morning. We passed by a number of locations for the TV show *True Blood* as we drove through *Shreveport* on the way to the *Black Bayou Lake National Wildlife Refuge*, on the hunt for even more wildlife.

We made our way down to *New Orleans* just in time for Mardi Gras, when the whole city becomes one big party, with costumes, beads, and parades through the streets. Don't worry if you don't make it for the carnival, though—the French Quarter maintains a party atmosphere all year round. For a taste of real Creole food, try some gumbo or a po' boy at the *Gumbo Shop (630 St. Peter St.)* and then wash it down with a Hurricane cocktail at *Pat O'Brien's (718 St. Peter St.)*, one of *Bourbon Street*'s famous bars. If you're in the mood for something sweet, nothing beats some fresh beignets on the patio of the *Café Du Monde (800 Decatur St.)*, where you can watch street entertainers and listen to jazz bands in *Jackson Square*—make sure to dust off all the powdered sugar from your clothes afterward though. And if you're tempted to explore the darker side of the Big Easy, the *Voodoo Museum* has everything you need to know about the dark arts, or you can take a tour of one of the city's beautiful cemeteries, where voodoo ceremonies still take place.

A Hurricane cocktail from Pat O'Brien's. One's more than enough!

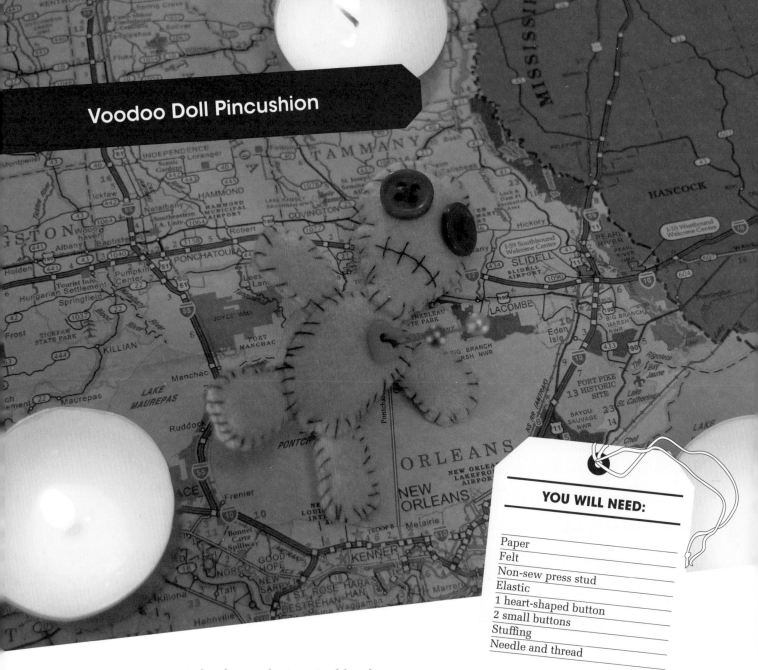

Voodoo Doll Pincushion

YOU WILL NEED:

Paper
Felt
Non-sew press stud
Elastic
1 heart-shaped button
2 small buttons
Stuffing
Needle and thread

A fun keepsake inspired by the
Voodoo Museum and graveyards
of New Orleans.

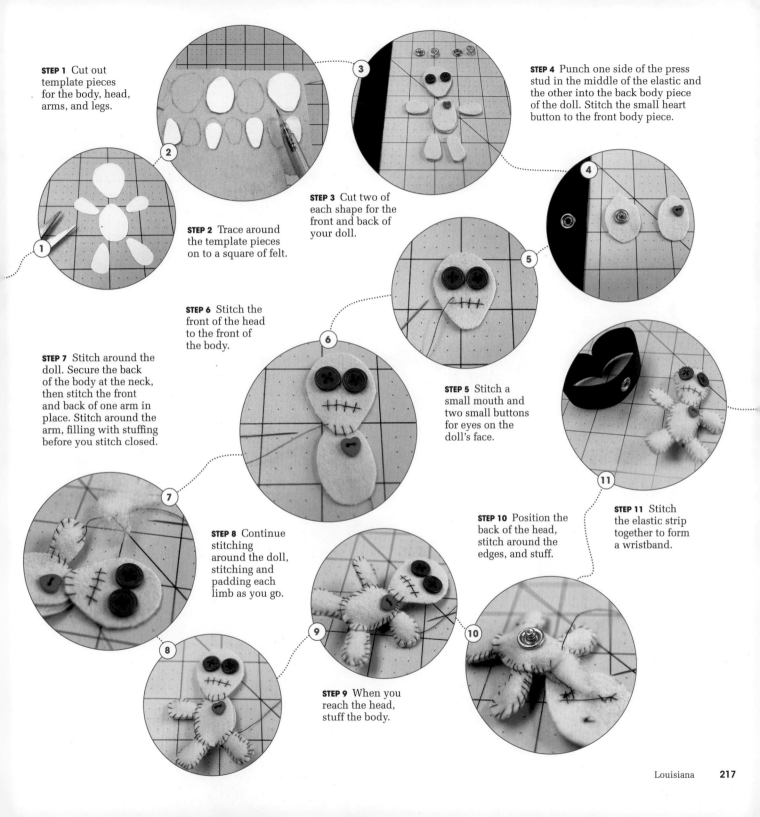

STEP 1 Cut out template pieces for the body, head, arms, and legs.

STEP 2 Trace around the template pieces on to a square of felt.

STEP 3 Cut two of each shape for the front and back of your doll.

STEP 4 Punch one side of the press stud in the middle of the elastic and the other into the back body piece of the doll. Stitch the small heart button to the front body piece.

STEP 5 Stitch a small mouth and two small buttons for eyes on the doll's face.

STEP 6 Stitch the front of the head to the front of the body.

STEP 7 Stitch around the doll. Secure the back of the body at the neck, then stitch the front and back of one arm in place. Stitch around the arm, filling with stuffing before you stitch closed.

STEP 8 Continue stitching around the doll, stitching and padding each limb as you go.

STEP 9 When you reach the head, stuff the body.

STEP 10 Position the back of the head, stitch around the edges, and stuff.

STEP 11 Stitch the elastic strip together to form a wristband.

Eating some fried shrimp and catfish at Delta Bistro, Greenwood.

Sleeping in a cotton picker's shack at Tallahatchie Flats.

A quick ride on the tractor, Tallahatchie Flats.

Bridges across the Yazoo River, Greenwood.

Teddy and grizzly bears at the Onward Store.

A mason jar light at Delta Bistro.

Art on a junction box in Jackson.

Mississippi

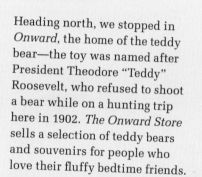

Heading north from Louisiana, we made our way through the Hospitality State, where the locals we met sure lived up to its reputation. Passing by a telephone tower disguised as the Washington Monument, we stopped for breakfast in *Jackson* before heading to *Vicksburg*, the town where Coca-Cola was first bottled and which appeared in the movie *O Brother, Where Art Thou?* Standing next to the calmly flowing Mississippi and looking at the historical waterline markings on the levee left us in awe of how high the river can get.

Heading north, we stopped in *Onward*, the home of the teddy bear—the toy was named after President Theodore "Teddy" Roosevelt, who refused to shoot a bear while on a hunting trip here in 1902. *The Onward Store* sells a selection of teddy bears and souvenirs for people who love their fluffy bedtime friends.

POST | CARD

The scenery became idyllic as we made our way farther north through picturesque cotton fields to *Greenwood*, although our thoughts soon turned to the slaves who once spent many back-breaking days here. We got to experience a little of their lives with a night at the *Tallahatchie Flats (58458 Country Rd. 518)*, where a number of donated cotton-picker's shacks from across the country have been turned into a motel.

The shacks retain their rustic charm and there's nothing better than sitting on the porch while watching the sunset. As we had heard from the owner, "If it ain't fried, it ain't food," so we were pleased to round off our trip with some fried catfish at the *Delta Bistro (117 Main St.)*.

A marker explaining the origin of the teddy bear.

Steamboat Coasters

Inspired by the steamboats on the Mississippi River and the rustic charm of our shack at the Tallahatchie Flats, these twine coasters are sure to make your guests feel like they're in the Hospitality State.

YOU WILL NEED:

Thin twine
C-2 (2.75mm) crochet hook
Spray starch (optional)

This project uses US terminology. For a table of UK terms, please see page 240.

STEP 1 Using thin twine, chain (ch) 6.

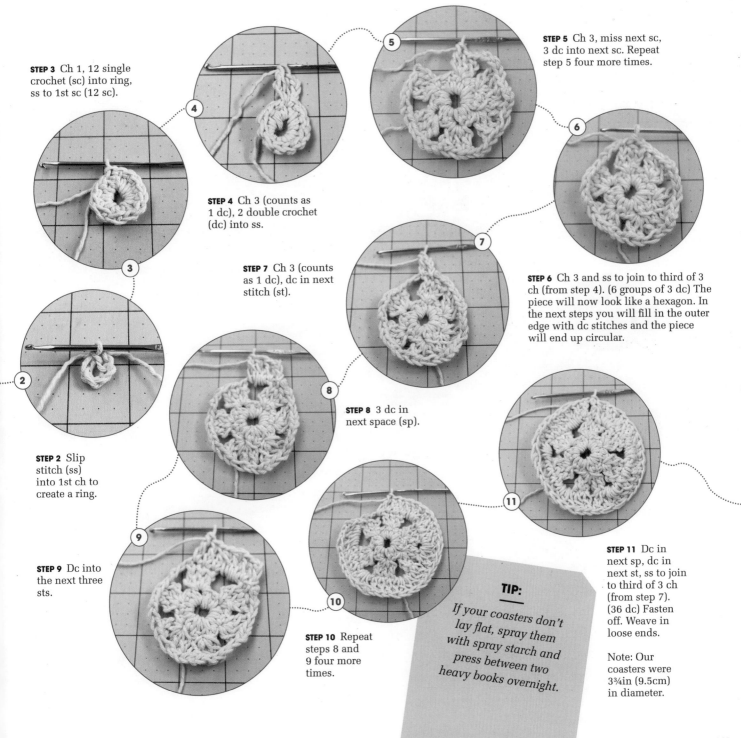

STEP 3 Ch 1, 12 single crochet (sc) into ring, ss to 1st sc (12 sc).

STEP 4 Ch 3 (counts as 1 dc), 2 double crochet (dc) into ss.

STEP 5 Ch 3, miss next sc, 3 dc into next sc. Repeat step 5 four more times.

STEP 6 Ch 3 and ss to join to third of 3 ch (from step 4). (6 groups of 3 dc) The piece will now look like a hexagon. In the next steps you will fill in the outer edge with dc stitches and the piece will end up circular.

STEP 7 Ch 3 (counts as 1 dc), dc in next stitch (st).

STEP 2 Slip stitch (ss) into 1st ch to create a ring.

STEP 8 3 dc in next space (sp).

STEP 9 Dc into the next three sts.

STEP 10 Repeat steps 8 and 9 four more times.

STEP 11 Dc in next sp, dc in next st, ss to join to third of 3 ch (from step 7). (36 dc) Fasten off. Weave in loose ends.

Note: Our coasters were 3¾in (9.5cm) in diameter.

TIP:

If your coasters don't lay flat, spray them with spray starch and press between two heavy books overnight.

Posters on display at Hatch Show Print, Nashville.

BB King's Blues Club on Beale Street, Nashville.

We loved Moon Pies—two biscuits filled with marshmallow. They're popular around here!

The Chattanooga Choo Choo at the old station, downtown Chattanooga.

A wall of singing fish at the Billy Bass Adoption Center, Memphis.

Hunting for bargains at Katy K's, Nashville.

Elvis at the start of his career on Beale Street, Memphis.

Tennessee

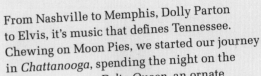

From Nashville to Memphis, Dolly Parton to Elvis, it's music that defines Tennessee. Chewing on Moon Pies, we started our journey in *Chattanooga*, spending the night on the *Delta Queen*, an ornate 1920s steamboat. The city is famous for another mode of transport, the *Chattanooga Choo Choo*, after the catchy song of the same name listed the destinations of the express train from New York.

We loved *Nashville*, and the bars and bands of Broadway. After a drink at the honky-tonk *Tootsies Orchid Lounge (422 Bdwy.)*, we swung by *Hatch Show Print (224 5th Ave. S.)*, a screen-printing shop with lovely cats roaming among the prints. If we'd been short of a cowboy boot or two, *Katy K's (2407 12th Ave. S.)* would have been the place to pick up everything vintage and Western.

Down the *Music Highway* (where even the rest stops are named after country and blues stars), we headed to *Memphis*. Country music makes way for the blues, and the bustling *Beale Street* is lined with bars and clubs. With Elvis's *Graceland* mansion nearby, there's no escaping the King of Rock 'n' Roll; 600,000 visitors a year come to tour the house, and his bedroom has been left untouched since 1977. After admiring some jumpsuits, you can see the pink cadillac, and even his private planes.

A Memphis Music neon sign, Beale Street.

We really felt the Southern way of life (and drawl) creep in, and after a homestyle breakfast we spotted the *Billy Bass Adoption Center (105 S. 2nd St.)*, a collection of the singing fish toys popular in the early 2000s. We were glad none of them were switched on!

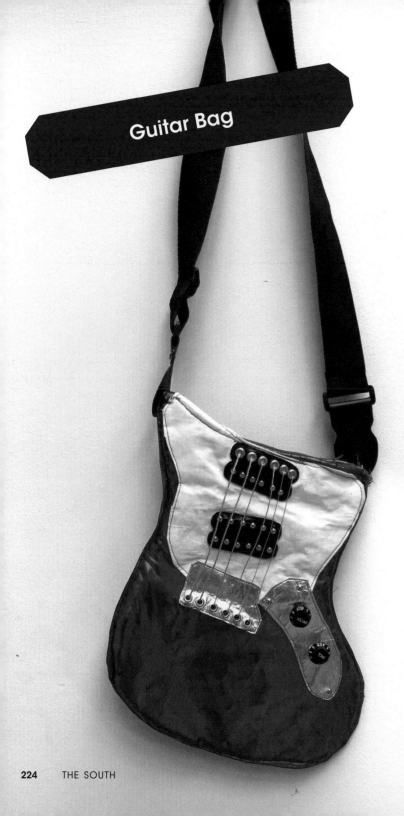

Guitar Bag

In the home of so much music, having an instrument like this on hand is no bad thing. It can be made in the style of any guitar, so pick your favorite model, get sketching, then head on down to the honky-tonk!

YOU WILL NEED:

Paper
Stabilizer
Shiny red fabric
White cotton
Shiny silver fabric
Black leather
12 large eyelets
21 small studs
Silver string in 3 different widths
Lining fabric
12in (30.5cm) red zipper
2 chunky buttons
Guitar strap
Volume and tone guitar knobs (available cheaply at most music stores)
Sewing machine and zipper foot
Chalk pencil
Eyelet punch
Heavy-duty needle
Hot-glue gun

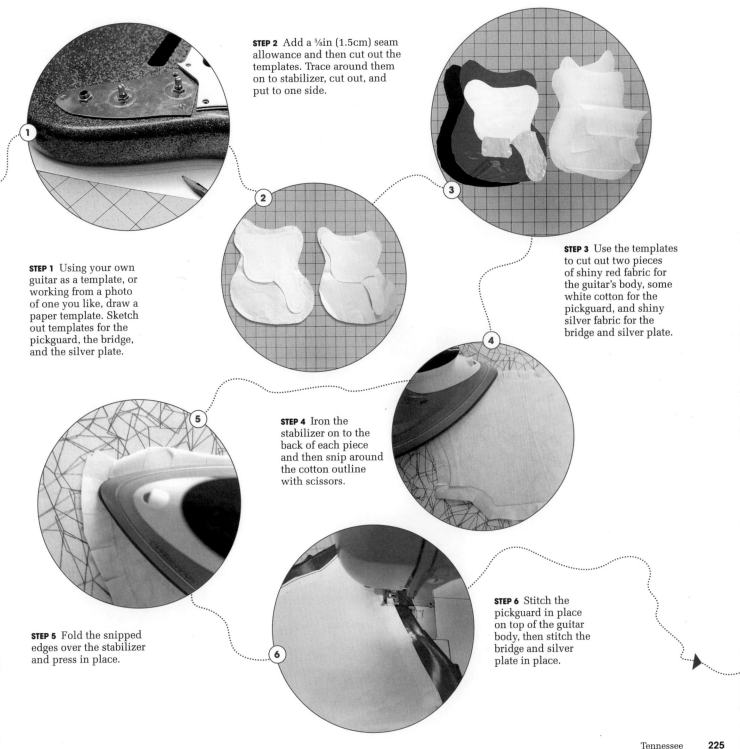

STEP 2 Add a ⅝in (1.5cm) seam allowance and then cut out the templates. Trace around them on to stabilizer, cut out, and put to one side.

STEP 1 Using your own guitar as a template, or working from a photo of one you like, draw a paper template. Sketch out templates for the pickguard, the bridge, and the silver plate.

STEP 3 Use the templates to cut out two pieces of shiny red fabric for the guitar's body, some white cotton for the pickguard, and shiny silver fabric for the bridge and silver plate.

STEP 4 Iron the stabilizer on to the back of each piece and then snip around the cotton outline with scissors.

STEP 5 Fold the snipped edges over the stabilizer and press in place.

STEP 6 Stitch the pickguard in place on top of the guitar body, then stitch the bridge and silver plate in place.

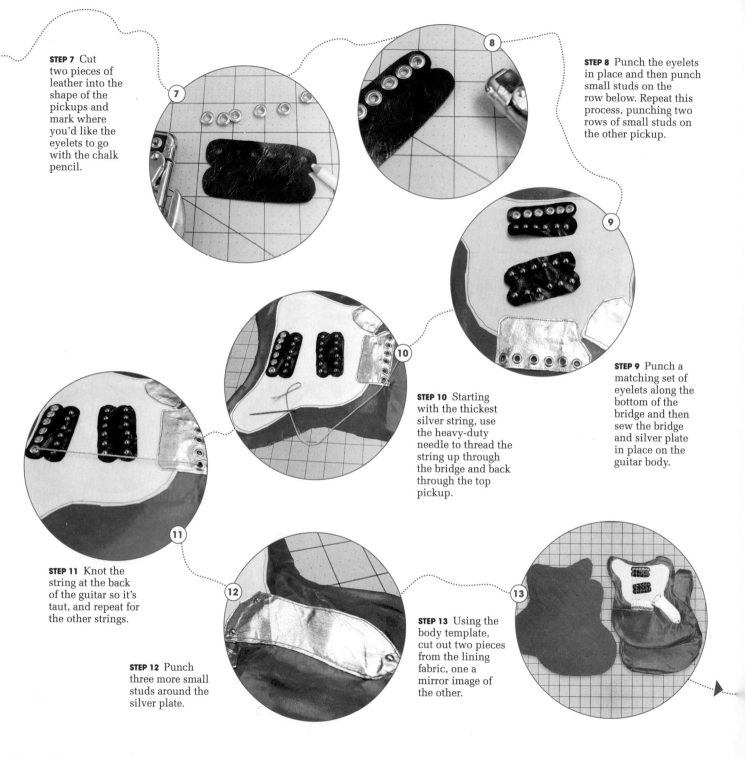

STEP 7 Cut two pieces of leather into the shape of the pickups and mark where you'd like the eyelets to go with the chalk pencil.

STEP 8 Punch the eyelets in place and then punch small studs on the row below. Repeat this process, punching two rows of small studs on the other pickup.

STEP 9 Punch a matching set of eyelets along the bottom of the bridge and then sew the bridge and silver plate in place on the guitar body.

STEP 10 Starting with the thickest silver string, use the heavy-duty needle to thread the string up through the bridge and back through the top pickup.

STEP 11 Knot the string at the back of the guitar so it's taut, and repeat for the other strings.

STEP 12 Punch three more small studs around the silver plate.

STEP 13 Using the body template, cut out two pieces from the lining fabric, one a mirror image of the other.

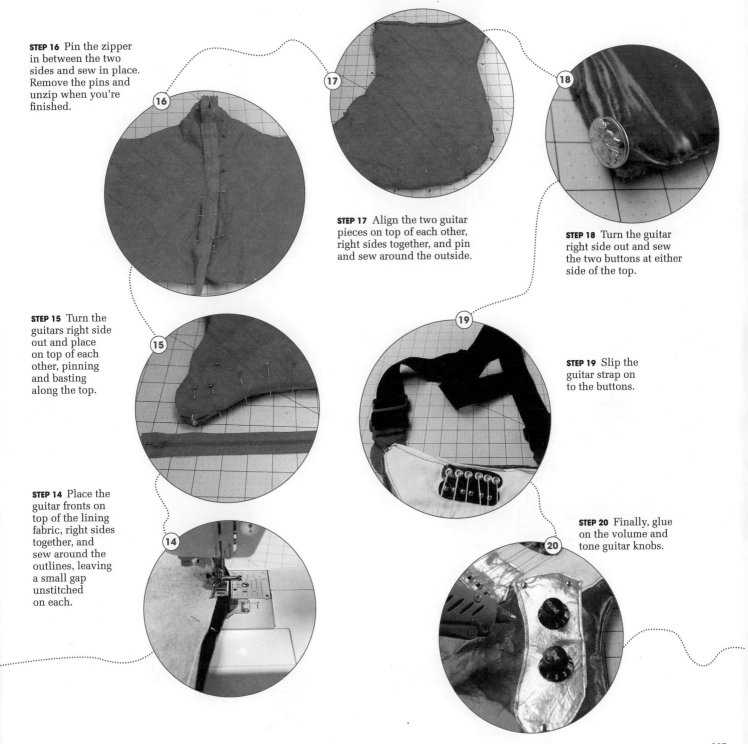

STEP 16 Pin the zipper in between the two sides and sew in place. Remove the pins and unzip when you're finished.

STEP 17 Align the two guitar pieces on top of each other, right sides together, and pin and sew around the outside.

STEP 18 Turn the guitar right side out and sew the two buttons at either side of the top.

STEP 15 Turn the guitars right side out and place on top of each other, pinning and basting along the top.

STEP 19 Slip the guitar strap on to the buttons.

STEP 14 Place the guitar fronts on top of the lining fabric, right sides together, and sew around the outlines, leaving a small gap unstitched on each.

STEP 20 Finally, glue on the volume and tone guitar knobs.

Horses in Bardstown.

Hillbilly Tea in Louisville brew their own moonshine alongside regular tea.

Learning about bourbon production at Jim Beam.

The Kentucky State Capitol, Frankfort.

Booker Noe, master distiller, at the Jim Beam Stillhouse.

Our night in the Jailer's Inn—in a cell! The last inmate left in 1987.

Somebody ended up in the stocks outside the Jailer's Inn.

KENTUCKY

WELCOME TO
Kentucky
UNBRIDLED SPIRIT™
Steven L. Beshear, Governor
Birthplace of Abraham Lincoln

The Bluegrass State is famous for its music, horses, and bourbon whiskey. After a quick tour of the *State Capitol Building (700 Capital Ave. Bay)* in *Frankfort*, where we admired the doll collection of governors' wives (complete with accurate inaugural dresses), we headed to *Louisville*. The super-hipster *Hillbilly Tea (120 S. 1st St.)* serves amazing food, alongside moonshine cocktails. However, the most famous food has to be Kentucky Fried Chicken, perfected by Colonel Sanders in 1940; more than 18,000 restaurants now sell the secret recipe, and a waxwork Colonel (complete with a bucket) greets guests at the *Visitors Center*.

The production of Kentucky bourbon is centered around the picturesque town of *Bardstown*, with four distilleries nearby. We stayed at the *Jailer's Inn (111 W. Stephen Foster Ave.)*, which was used to lock up prisoners behind 30in (75cm)-thick walls from 1797 until 1987. We appreciated that they kept the stories of hauntings until the next morning, after a delicious breakfast in the courtyard. We also took a free tour of *Jim Beam*, and learned what it takes to make a Kentucky bourbon. The distilled corn must age for at least two years in a new, oak-charred barrel. Luckily, they'd made some earlier, so we sampled it fresh from the bottle.

Fried food and alcohol aren't the only things that Kentucky has spread worldwide. "Happy Birthday To You" was written in Louisville, the Post-it note was invented in *Cynthiana*, and the Louisville Slugger baseball bat whacks home runs across the country. And don't forget bluegrass music, Mohammed Ali, and Abraham Lincoln!

Our last stop was *Fort Knox*, where the US Bullion Depository stores around 200 billion dollars of gold bars. There isn't a visitor center, and the tank parked outside sends a message—it's locked up tighter than, urm, Fort Knox!

Give the Colonel a run for his money with your very own secret sauce. It'll taste so good, you'll put your name on it!

A good condiment can be the difference between okay-ish, and finger-licking.

Each area of the US does things a little differently. Our starting point is a Kentucky black barbeque sauce; the addition of Worcestershire sauce gives it a lovely kick.

Other sauces start off with a tomato sauce, brown sauce, or even a mayonnaise base. Whatever you start with is up to you. Taste as you go, and don't be afraid to experiment.

Secret Sauce

FOR A BLACK BARBEQUE SAUCE BASE:

¼ cup (30g) minced onion
oil, for frying
¼ cup (60ml) white vinegar
½ cup (120ml) Worcestershire sauce
1 tsp brown sugar

TO MAKE IT YOUR OWN:

Black pepper
Lemon juice
Paprika
Nutmeg
Tabasco
Cayenne pepper
Sea salt

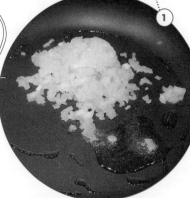

STEP 1 Fry the onion until soft with a little oil.

STEP 2 Add the vinegar and Worcestershire sauce.

STEP 3 Keep simmering and add the sugar. Now, get creative! What you've got so far won't taste great, so add some of the optional ingredients until it's just right.

STEP 4 Pour the sauce through a sieve into a sterilized bottle and label it. You can keep it as a table sauce, or use it as a marinade.

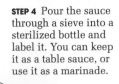

SECRET SAUCE

A shack at the Sloss Furnaces in Birmingham.

Old iron-smelting equipment at Sloss Furnaces, Birmingham.

Lunch at the train-wreck-themed Derailed Diner, Robertsdale.

The Birmingham skyline from Vulcan Park.

At the state line.

The 56ft (17m)-tall Vulcan statue in Vulcan Park, Birmingham.

Milkshake at Flip Burger Boutique.

ALABAMA

When the highway Welcome Center has a rocking chair on the porch, you'll know you've hit Alabama! Known for hospitality and Southern charm, you'll be feeling at home almost as soon as you cross into the Heart of Dixie.

Our first stop was the Magic City, *Birmingham*. The iron and steel industry of the area is represented by the largest cast-iron sculpture in the world, *Vulcan*, which overlooks the city. We stopped for gourmet burgers, milkshakes, and sweet potato tots at the super hipster *Flip Burger Boutique (220 Summit Blvd.)*.

Afterward we took a tour of the *Sloss Furnaces*, an old iron-making furnace that has been turned into a national landmark for the public to explore freely. Keep an eye out for the golden *Miss Elektra* statue when exploring downtown, too.

POST | CARD

Along the highway in *Tuscaloosa*, we found a sleeping robot on the grass at the *University of Alabama*. The city was hit by a tornado in 2011, and you can see several souvenirs from survivors around the town, including a tree stump and the blinking *Moon Winx Lodge* sign on *University Blvd.*, whose neon was all but removed during the storm. Down south in *Robertsdale* we stopped for dinner at the *Derailed Diner (27801 County Road 64)*, a drive-in restaurant that fans of trains and eccentricity will love.

Y'all make sure to visit, ok?

The Moon Winx Lodge sign in Tuscaloosa, complete with blinking eyes!

Sweet Tea Mason Jars

Customize some glass jars as a nod to the iconic Mason preserving jar and fill with Alabama's favorite drink—sweet tea. It's the perfect refresher for a hot summer day.

YOU WILL NEED:

Glass jars with lids
Eyelets (large enough for a straw to slip through)
Sticker paper
Chalkboard paint
Straws
Drill
Craft knife
Paintbrush

GET CREATIVE:

Mix up the recipe by using your favorite flavor of tea.

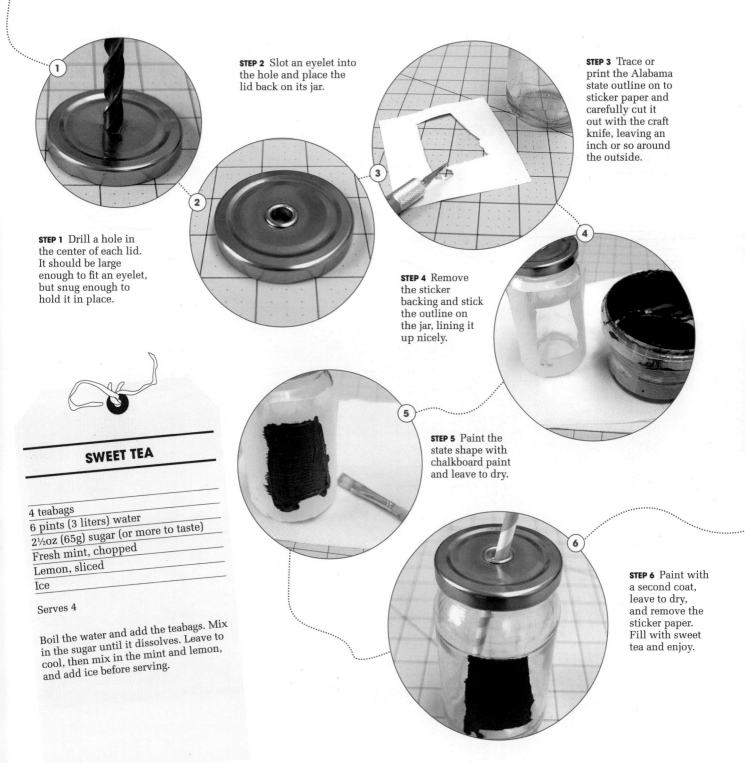

STEP 1 Drill a hole in the center of each lid. It should be large enough to fit an eyelet, but snug enough to hold it in place.

STEP 2 Slot an eyelet into the hole and place the lid back on its jar.

STEP 3 Trace or print the Alabama state outline on to sticker paper and carefully cut it out with the craft knife, leaving an inch or so around the outside.

STEP 4 Remove the sticker backing and stick the outline on the jar, lining it up nicely.

STEP 5 Paint the state shape with chalkboard paint and leave to dry.

STEP 6 Paint with a second coat, leave to dry, and remove the sticker paper. Fill with sweet tea and enjoy.

SWEET TEA

4 teabags

6 pints (3 liters) water

2½oz (65g) sugar (or more to taste)

Fresh mint, chopped

Lemon, sliced

Ice

Serves 4

Boil the water and add the teabags. Mix in the sugar until it dissolves. Leave to cool, then mix in the mint and lemon, and add ice before serving.

Horse and cart tours around Savannah.

The Thunderbird Inn motel, Savannah.

Railroad trestle in Athens, which appeared as artwork on R.E.M.'s first album.

Fountains in a garden square, downtown Savannah.

Late-night dessert and cocktails at Lulu's Chocolate Bar.

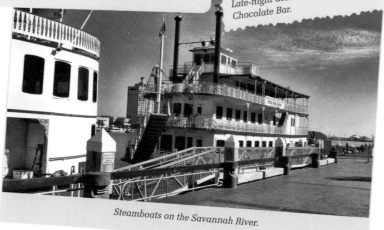
Steamboats on the Savannah River.

Johnny Mercer wrote lyrics to 1,500 songs, including "Moon River." This statue of him stands in Ellis Square.

Georgia

From mountains and forests to beaches and swamps, Georgia is one of the most diverse states, sure to keep your eye stimulated as you drive from city to city while keeping count of the number of peaches you spot on road signs.

We started in the state capital, *Atlanta*—home of Coca-Cola, CNN, and host of the 1996 Olympics. Although downtown can be busy and touristy, the *Little Five Points* neighborhood to the east is sure to please the crafty and creative, with a wide range of record stores, bars, bookstores, and coffee shops. We browsed zines and music at *Criminal Records (1154 Euclid Ave. NE)*, grabbed burgers at *The Vortex* *(438 Moreland Ave.)*, and enjoyed the triple bill at the *Starlight Six drive-in (2000 Moreland Ave. SE)*.

The next day we headed east to *Athens*, an arty college town famous for its music scene, to visit the *Tree That Owns Itself (cnr. South Finley & Dearing)* and grab lunch at *The Grit (199 Prince Ave.)*, a restaurant associated with bands such as R.E.M.

We then drove 225 miles (360km) southeast to *Savannah*, a historic city on the coast. Make sure to bring your camera, as you'll want to take photos of the gorgeous buildings, cemeteries, and eerie Spanish moss hanging from the trees. After spending the night at the retro-kitsch *Thunderbird Inn (611 W. Oglethorpe Ave.)*, we sampled the pralines on *River Street*, grabbed breakfast at *The Sentient Bean (13 E. Park Ave.)* overlooking the beautiful fountains in *Forsyth Park*, tucked into late-night cake and cocktails at *Lulu's Chocolate Bar (42 Martin Luther King Jr. Blvd.)*, and almost went on a hearse-driven ghost tour. We also headed south from the city to *Okefenokee Swamp Park*, where we spotted an alligator, and *Crooked River State Park*, where we cycled through the forest on a tandem.

Okefenokee Swamp Park, south Georgia.

Bacon Bit Pralines

We first tasted pralines on the riverfront in Savannah, where dozens of candy stores lure tourists in with free samples.

Pralines are small candy disks made from pecans and caramelized sugar. Sure to please any sweet tooth, we've combined ours with bacon bits to create an all-American treat!

INGREDIENTS:

7oz (200g) superfine (caster) sugar
4oz (110g) brown sugar
1 cup (225ml) milk
3 tbsp butter
1 tsp vanilla extract
3½oz (100g) pecans
3 tbsp bacon bits (we used a meat-free bacon)
Cookie sheet (baking tray)
Candy thermometer (optional)

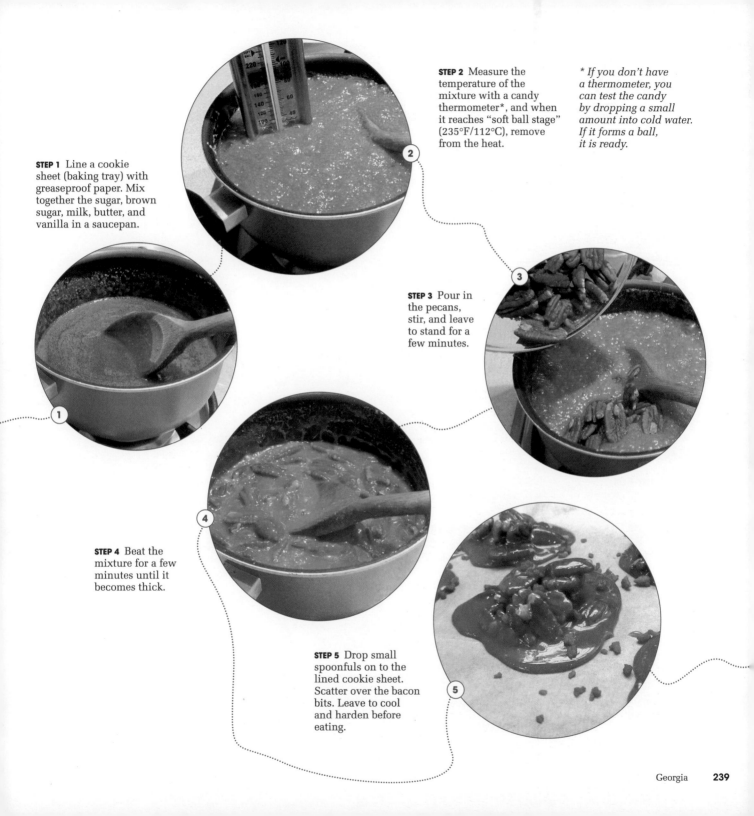

STEP 1 Line a cookie sheet (baking tray) with greaseproof paper. Mix together the sugar, brown sugar, milk, butter, and vanilla in a saucepan.

STEP 2 Measure the temperature of the mixture with a candy thermometer*, and when it reaches "soft ball stage" (235°F/112°C), remove from the heat.

If you don't have a thermometer, you can test the candy by dropping a small amount into cold water. If it forms a ball, it is ready.

STEP 3 Pour in the pecans, stir, and leave to stand for a few minutes.

STEP 4 Beat the mixture for a few minutes until it becomes thick.

STEP 5 Drop small spoonfuls on to the lined cookie sheet. Scatter over the bacon bits. Leave to cool and harden before eating.

Project Index

Crochet and knitting terminology

Crochet

US	UK
single crochet (sc)	double crochet (dc)
double crochet (dc)	treble crochet (tr)
treble (tr)	double treble (dtr)

Knitting

US	UK
seed stitch	moss stitch
stockinette stitch	stocking stitch
bind off	cast off